WHY NOT?
Priesthood & the
Ministry of Women

WHY NOT?

Priesthood & the Ministry of Women

A theological study edited by
MICHAEL BRUCE & G. E. DUFFIELD

The Marcham Manor Press
Appleford Abingdon Berkshire
Sutton Courtenay 319

CONTRIBUTORS

R. T. BECKWITH Librarian of Latimer House, Oxford.
Church of England

G. G. BLUM Lecturer in Early Church Studies, Philipps-Universitat, Marburg.
Evangelical Church in Germany

The late MICHAEL BRUCE, for many years Proctor in Canterbury Convocation. EDITOR
Church of England

HANS CAVALLIN Member of the Swedish Brotherhood of the Holy Cross and New Testament specialist.
Church of Sweden

G. E. DUFFIELD Editor of News Extra and Member of General Synod. EDITOR
Church of England

E. R. HARDY University Lecturer in the Faculty of Divinity, Cambridge.
Protestant Episcopal Church, USA

E. L. MASCALL Professor of Historical Theology, King's College, London.
Church of England

J. I. PACKER Associate Principal, Trinity College, Bristol.
Church of England

J. J. VON ALLMEN Professor of Practical Theology, University of Neuchâtel.
Swiss Reformed Church

C. D. W. ROBINSON St. Edmund Hall, Oxford translated Professor von Allmen's essay.

© Marcham Manor Press, 1972

CONTENTS

Preface	6
Feminism and the Church *G.E.Duffield*	9
The Office of Woman in the Church to the Present Day *R.T.Beckwith*	26
Heresy, Equality and the Rights of Women *M.Bruce*	40
The Priestess in the Greco-Roman World *E.R.Hardy*	56
The Office of Woman in the New Testament *G.G.Blum*	63
Representative Priesthood? *J.I.Packer*	78
Demythologising the Liberal Illusion *H.Cavallin*	81
Women and the Priesthood of the Church *E.L.Mascall*	95
Women and the Threefold Ministry *J.J.von Allmen translated by C.D.W.Robinson*	121
Towards a Better Solution *R.T.Beckwith and G.E.Duffield*	132

PREFACE

G. E. Duffield

WHEN C. S. LEWIS HEARD that Anglicans were considering the possibility of ordaining women, he wrote:

> At first sight all the rationality . . . is on the side of the innovators. We are short of priests. We have discovered in one profession after another that women can do very well all sorts of things which were once supposed to be in the power of men alone. No one among those who dislike the proposal is maintaining that women are less capable than men of piety, zeal, learning, and whatever else seems necessary for the pastoral office. What, then, except prejudice begotten by tradition, forbids us to draw on the huge reserves which could pour into the priesthood if women were here as in so many other professions, put on the same footing as men? And against this flood of commonsense, the opposers (many of them women) can produce at first nothing but an inarticulate distaste, a sense of discomfort which they themselves find it hard to analyse. (*Undeceptions*, p.192)

This book represents a cooperative attempt by Christians from very diverse denominational and theological traditions and different countries to set out the theological objections to ordination of women to the presbyterate. We believe Lewis was right. A great many people feel instinctively that there is something wrong about this possibility even though some other churches have ordained women (never on a large scale and rarely to any but the most obscure positions), and this symposium aims to give some theological reasons why such a course is not desirable, and at the end to suggest some better ways forward.

We have not sought to work out alternatives in detail, for such details would vary from church to church and from country to country. Our aim has rather been to consider the underlying theological issues, to give our reasons why the ordination of women to the priesthood is a mistaken solution to the question of the right place of women in the ministry of the Church, and then to offer outline alternatives.

The work had its origin some years back with the late Michael Bruce, and as far as the English contributors were concerned it was then planned as a largely catholic book. But when Michael discovered that evangelicals too felt doubts about ordaining women, he readily agreed to alter the project to include their contributions. Michael and I planned to edit the work jointly when death struck with unexpected suddenness, and I was left to replan on my own. I believed it right to keep to Michael's plan for a joint evangelical-catholic venture, and I wish to thank Roger Beckwith for his considerable help in re-constituting the work. It is only fair to add that some of the original contributions were written a few years back, but I trust that others of more recent origin have done any updating necessary. Some may comment cynically on the fact that all the contributors are men. To that I reply that both Michael and I worked on the basis that the quality of the contribution was what mattered, the expertise not the sex of its author. I can assure any doubting feminists that we have consulted women widely in the course of preparing the volume.

For myself, and no one amongst our contributors is committed to anything except what appears over his own name, I want to add a word of explanation about this joint catholic-evangelical venture. I rejoice greatly that evangelicals and catholics within the Church of England are able to work happily together. Of course there remain theological differences, but I believe some of them are diminishing, and there is certainly an increasing desire to discuss them freely and amicably, and notwithstanding the differences there is a common and growing realisation of theological agreement on many basic essentials of our faith. It grieves me somewhat that some churchmen who a few years ago were lamenting the continuing controversy between catholics and evangelicals today seem to disparage their newly discovered friendship. I believe that such fellowship and friendship will grow, and hope that cynical critics will cease attributing that cooperation to base motives and believe fellow Christians capable of theological integrity. When as I trust will soon be the case such cooperation extends to pastoral matters, I hope accusations such as unholy alliances and expediency will be dropped. It will be seen in this book that catholics and evangelicals have worked together harmoniously and each has been free to work on his own presuppositions.

Finally I should like to pay a tribute to Michael Bruce himself. As a very young member of Church Assembly and half Michael's age, and though we were from very diverse Anglican traditions, I warmed greatly to Michael. He was courtesy itself in trying to understand other viewpoints: he always took theology seriously and it was characteristic of him that he readily agreed to alter a previously planned book to meet another viewpoint.

Note: one word about the style of the book. There are a few slight inconsistencies of style due to parts of this work being set up in type much earlier. Acknowledgment is due to the Church Union for permission to reproduce with slight revisions Dr. Mascall's chapter, and also to E. J. Brill of Leyden for Dr. Blum's article which first appeared in German in one of their publications.

Feminism and the Church

GERVASE E. DUFFIELD

IT IS FREQUENTLY ARGUED today that women have at last achieved, or almost achieved, their rightful place of equality with men. They have come a long way in the twentieth century. In British politics neither Tories nor Socialists appoint a cabinet without at least one woman. Israel has a woman prime minister, so have India and Ceylon. In most western countries women are now found as company directors, doctors, professors (even professors of theology), lawyers, judges, and so on. Why then have the churches, specifically the Roman, Orthodox, almost all Anglican and some Reformed churches, together with most evangelical independent churches, lagged so far behind? Newspapers and secular sources press the question. (Kenneth Hudson in *Men & Women*, p. 21, actually says, 'The Church Assembly is a strong candidate for the title of the most anti-feminist body in Britain.') Why are not women ordained on an equality with men? So runs the common argument in church circles, and it illustrates the nature of the pressure to have women ordained; it need hardly be added that ecumenical pronouncements (especially those from the Ecumenical Press Service in Geneva) constantly hint in this direction. Our intention here is to look at these pressures, together with their background, and then analyse out the right questions for Christians to ask in the current debate. There is a growing tendency to say that there are 'no conclusive theological' arguments against ordaining women, but for various 'other reasons' (until recently) the time has not been thought ripe for such an act in most churches. Now the word *conclusive* is being quietly dropped and the *other reasons*, always a bit vague, are melting away. Is it simply a matter of time before the churches catch up with the dominant mood of the western world? And is this the right way for Christians to approach the problem?

Christianity and women in history

OUR Lord himself undoubtedly raised the status of women in the ancient world. He broke the bondage of current convention (e.g. the woman at the well in Jn. 4: 27); over marriage he went behind current Rabbinic disputes, and even past the Mosaic divorce exception for hardness of heart, though he did not condemn that, to the pristine purity of Genesis (Mt. 19); and both Luke and Acts show women prominent among his followers. Currently it is widely and erroneously thought that Paul reversed this attitude, substituting for it male domination and a view of marriage as second best to celibacy.[1] But in considering modern needs the Christian should be aware of the honourable record of women in church history, from the many martyrs, saints and nuns in the early days (too numerous to relate), through the ladies of the Reformation (Renée Duchess of Ferrara greatly helped Calvin, Jeanne d'Albret played no small part in aiding the Huguenots, Marguerite of Navarre wrote high class mystical poetry, Julia Gonzaga was prominent in the Valdesian circle in Italy which included Reformers and reforming Romans like Contarini and Sadoleto, Queen Elizabeth translated theology as did Lady Ann Bacon, translator of Jewel's *Apology*), up to the nineteenth century, which saw a host of Christian women pioneering social reform, the Quaker Elizabeth Fry in prisons, and the Anglicans Hannah More and Josephine Butler in education and reform of the prostitution laws.

Feminism

THE starting point of British feminism* is normally taken to be Mary Wollstonecraft's book *A Vindication of the Rights of Women* first published in 1792. Mary became something of a feminist hero later, but in her own day and for a good while afterwards, she was (if widely commented upon) universally disparaged, castigated and mocked. Following Tom Paine's *The Rights of Man* and Mary's own chaotic life, living with several men, suicide attempts, etc., it is hardly surprising that she had little positive influence, and her ideas were treated much as other ideas culled from the French Revolution had been (Mary went over to France, observing and studying events there).

The real development came in the nineteenth century. The rapid change begun by the industrial revolution brought the population more and more from agricultural work in the countryside to industrial work in the towns. Family responsibilities still remained of course, but

*The word is used here without overtones and in a broad sense to cover the whole range of concern for feminine equality. In modern contexts it comes to mean a more aggressive egalitarianism in some cases, since votes and higher education for women are now history, and the militancy of Women's Lib. is upon us.

women ceased to help on the land and instead worked long hours in the new factories and down the mines. They then went home to do their domestic duties far into the night and even through the night. That was intolerable, as leaders like Shaftesbury soon appreciated, but the new factory work did have the byproduct of giving women a new standing in the family as part wage earner. Upper class ladies were still escaping from Georgian life that was in the words of Katharine Moore 'very idle and empty-headed'[2] and was satirised in Pope's *The Rape of the Lock*. But feminist leadership, and indeed support, was middle class. John Stuart Mill was to become, after his conversion to feminism through his wife, one of the leaders of the feminist nineteenth century thrust. It was from about the middle of the century that the breakthrough came. In 1857 women were allowed to divorce for cruelty or desertion. In 1869 Mill wrote *The Subjection of Women*, the feminist's Bible. In 1888 the first woman was elected to the London City Council. Meanwhile in 1865 Elizabeth Garrett Anderson had become the first woman doctor. In 1907 Hyde Park witnessed the first open air women's suffrage rally, and in 1918 women were given the vote. Between the wars the feminist causes waned, partly because most objectives were achieved, partly through sheer exhaustion, and partly through disillusionment that goals achieved had not brought the feminist utopia some had expected.

In America feminism was a nineteenth century development, but it flourished earlier than in Britain. American women had always had a great passion for organising themselves into feminine groups, and this situation extended back to the early part of the century, providing a ready platform from which women could voice their opinions. The organisations were innumerable and covered every conceivable charitable and moral purpose, from education and suffrage to temperance and anti-slavery.

Many American women were drawn into the suffrage cause through their concern to get the female vote for some other cause close to their hearts. Early on feminism was linked with the crusade against slavery. Among the pioneers were the Grimké sisters. In 1838 Sarah wrote a book, *Letters on the Equality of the Sexes and the Condition of Women*, answering the Congregationalist clergy of Massachusetts. She attacked slavery and asserted women's rights in church and society, basing a lot of her argument on biblical phrases. The first feminist gathering was the 1848 Seneca Falls Convention. It was a small and local affair yet significant for the future. Its declaration on women's rights was again based on the Bible, or at any rate couched in biblical phraseology, and Lucretia Mott put this resolution to the gathering:

> That the speedy success of our cause depends upon the zealous and untiring efforts of both men and women, for the overthrow of the monopoly of the pulpit, and for the securing to woman an equal participation with men in the various trades, professions and commerce.[3]

The feminist cause on both sides of the Atlantic followed a roughly similar pattern and even timetable. Feminists concentrated on getting higher education for girls. Oberlin College was the first higher educational institute in the USA to admit girls and produced the first female graduate in 1841. Queen's and Bedford Colleges were founded in 1848 and 1849. Girton College, Cambridge, was founded in 1869. Then feminists tended to concentrate on the vote, legal status of women in marriage, their property, and also a few specific issues like prostitution where double morality standards operated (infuriating Josephine Butler). There were many hints that marriage should be changed or even abolished, but no one quite had the temerity then to work out an alternative. This was to come later with Women's Lib. The one major difference between the sides of the Atlantic was that Prohibition was a feminist cause in the USA, but scarcely in Britain. In the 1890s there was an increase in feminist flirtations with free love, and sympathisers like Havelock Ellis were struggling to revise sexual *mores*, believing that thereby they would liberate women.

But in America as in Britain feminism died down between the wars. Its most recent US revival came in the 1960s when Betty Friedan published *The Feminine Mystique*, an attempt to get a better deal for American women in business and in social life.

Before we turn to look at Women's Liberation, it is worth trying to disentangle the two strands in feminism of the nineteenth and early twentieth century variety, though the distinction is never absolute. First, a relatively small group see feminism as a part of a total social revolution, almost invariably left-wing, against current morality, and established political, economic and social values. Such people tended to write revolutionary books but remained very small in numbers. Second, the overwhelming majority of feminists accepted conventional morality (note for instance how late contraception was accepted by feminists as a whole), but shared a solidarity with others of their sex in fighting for the vote and certain legal standards.

Victories won and opportunities lost

NINETEENTH century feminism won some victories the value of which few would dispute today. They achieved, for instance, the safeguarding of certain property rights for women, they contributed to the advance of higher education for women, they ultimately won the vote for women, they destroyed much of the double morality standards involved in prostitution legislation, and they demonstrated that in many professions women can in their own way do the job quite as well as men.

In education, in Britain as in America, girls do not seem to have taken full advantage of their new opportunities. Professor O'Neill shows that percentage-wise the number of women in higher education has actually gone down between the 1920s and the 1950s in USA, while Dr. Constance Rover notes, on the British scene, 'the disincentive to an effort which may well seem unproductive in view of the short period of work-anticipation before marriage'.[4] These educational trends, and V. A. Demant's section 5 in *Women & Holy Orders* (pp. 102 ff.), should make for caution before anyone assumes a total evolution of women's role in society. It is much more complex than that, and certainly no smooth evolutionary curve on the graph.

Women's Lib.

BETTY Friedan's *National Organisation of Women* belongs to the second stream of feminism, and according to Juliet Mitchell is not now regarded as part of Women's Lib.[5] Women's Lib. (WL) appeared in the late 1960s and without doubt belongs to the militant left-wing revolutionary strand in feminism, very much the minority strand in earlier feminism. WL reckons to start where the earlier feminists left off. They had achieved the vote and changed much of the law; educational opportunity has been greatly expanded (and no less important, contraception, RCs apart, is now almost universally accepted, thus reducing family responsibilities). None of that satisfies WL, who call for total revolution. Mitchell claims the movement is international, with branches in all the western liberal democracies except three: Iceland which she describes as remote, and Austria and Switzerland which she dismisses as socially the most traditional countries. She repudiates the charge that WL is predominantly American. She does not rule out the use of violence in future; she resents the laughter with which WL is often treated, but with the unhistorical romanticism not uncommon in the revolutionary she insists WL is something essentially new and 'the most revolutionary movement ever to have existed'.[6]

She traces WL's emergence with other revolutionary groups of the late '60s, the students, Black Power, Hippies. According to her, women gave up Black Power when Stokely Carmichael made plain that Black Power meant black men with black women at home, and she views racism as merely an offshoot of the far greater problem, sexism,[7] the WL term for male domination of women. She concedes WL's middle class origin and complexion; most of its leaders are graduates, all women—men are not trusted within it, the Stokeley Carmichael pontification apparently being a bitter disillusionment to these revolutionary women. She is convinced that WL must be totally revolutionary and that all revolutionaries must work together in a total attack on capitalism and its system. She asserts that arts students are in the van of WL; she does not identify them further but it is not hard to guess that they are the social science, politics and art students, and she recognises that the vast expansion in higher education in recent years has made such a movement possible. Whether this is the underprivileged seizing their opportunity, as she would like us to think, or a large number of people not being quite ready or up to the new educational openings, as others have said[8] and industry's increasing hesitation with these new graduates might suggest, is another matter. WL is seen as an urban phenomenon, and capitalism is blamed as the cause of the present 'general denigration of women' (p. 40). Her grievances are largely economic and legal, and occasionally biological. Abortion and contraception are demanded free for all. It is worth noting how attacks on capitalism, plus the demand for abortion and contraception, are now essential to the WL platform. Mitchell is anxious to show that WL is not still another form of feminine socialism, and she goes out of her way to demonstrate just how hidebound traditional European socialism has been towards women.[9] Women in short are exploited at work and relegated to the home by modern democracies, but modern technology will give them the chance: 'Industrial labour and automated technology both promise the preconditions for women's liberation alongside men's'. Contraception is vital to WL because childbearing must be totally voluntary, and then for every woman it 'becomes one option among others'.[10] WL is not just carrying on the old feminist struggles, says Miss Mitchell; it is waging all out war against capitalist society and attacking the whole concept of family life, as traditionally understood by Christians at any rate.

Miss Mitchell certainly writes with youthful enthusiasm, and we wonder just what would actually happen if she ever got control of anything important, but we also wondered if she is just an extremist in WL. We have looked extensively elsewhere. The same basic notions appear in Germaine Greer, *The Female Eunuch* (all but anarchist), in Kate Millett, *Sexual Politics* (historical survey with a left-wing framework), and in Shulamith Firestone, *The Dialectic of Sex*, among others. The last book is very recent, and works out the fullest WL alternative we have yet seen. Like Kate Miller, Miss Firestone is a young American and at 26 a leader of transatlantic WL. She concludes her book by making four demands prerequisite to any alternative system, and we quote her verbatim:[11]

'1. *The freeing of women from the tyranny of their reproductive biology by every means available, and the diffusion of the childbearing and childrearing role to the society as a whole, men as well as women.*' She goes on to dismiss things like day-care centres as 'timid, if not entirely worthless as a transition. We're talking about *radical* change'. She then talks about 'distant solutions based on the potentials of modern embryology', presumably a dark hint at test-tube babies.

'2. *The full self-determination, including economic independence, of both women and children.*' This means social and economic change, and we are back with the radical attack on capitalism. Women are the foundation of our economic superstructure, but this is concealed from them by means of praise about self-sacrificing motherhood, though without any basis in reality. 'We have now attacked the family on a double front, challenging that around which it is organised: reproduction of the species by females and its outgrowth, the physical dependence of women and children. To eliminate these would be enough to destroy the family, which breeds the power psychology.'

'3. *The total integration of women and children into all aspects of the larger society.* All institutions that segregate the sexes, or bar children from adult society, e.g., the modern school, must be destroyed.'

'4. *The freedom of all women and children to do whatever they wish to do sexually.* There will no longer be any reason *not* to.'

Even if the reader thinks this hopelessly 'utopian' and out of touch with social as well as feminine realities, he can at least admire the young lady for her consistency and courage to spell out exactly what is involved. It is not difficult to add it all up. Capitalism must go. The family is part of it, so that must go. Our schools break up society, so they go. Moral standards impinge on freedom, so they must go. One is tempted to ask what sort of strange anarchy would be left, but our task here is to expound WL and its implications, rather than criticise this 'utopia'.

Social developments and technical changes

WE have concentrated on post-1850 developments in feminism, because increasingly, and especially with WL, they have presented an ideological challenge to the Christian view of the family and the general male-female relationship in society, but in our enthusiasm we should not slip into the false assumption that there is one continuous evolutionary process of feminism. Feminism declined during the inter-war period, and the post-J. S. Mill age has witnessed some stridently anti-feminine voices like Kierkegaard and Strindberg. It is not a straight evolutionary process, as some assume, but as Dr. V. A. Demant writes, 'recognition of women's powers, abilities and influence is not the result of a historical progressive movement but comes and goes with certain cultures and attitudes'. Note should now be taken of modern sociological discussions. *Family Issues of Employed Women in Europe and America*[12] is a convenient book to take, not because it advances any startlingly new lines, but because it is very recent, challenges a number of common assumptions, and especially because it spans such a wide geographical and political range, Communist and Liberal-democratic countries, Europe and America. It is primarily about married women, but is nonetheless relevant to the possibility of ordaining women, for no one suggests that any future ordained women should be confined to celibacy.

First, E. Grønseth asks if the husband as family provider is as basic to the family idea as people commonly imagine. He rather doubts it, but what are the consequences if he is right? If the husband is not to be regarded as the breadwinner, is it right that legislation should make him largely responsible for any children in a divorce or a separation? If breadwinning is to be equally shared, what happens if the wife is so tied up with looking after young children that she cannot earn an income? That takes us on to the further issue as to how far a state ought to consider itself the essential provider of things like day-care centres where children can be left while a wife works. As with almost every Government matter, it is a question of budget priorities, but behind them must lie a state's belief, even if subconscious, as to whether it wants to encourage a society in which children are more and more the care of the community and in which it is agreed as a desirable goal that women should always be freed from such domestic responsibilities so that they can take ordinary jobs. Logically, if a state decides to encourage all women to go out to work, there will soon have to be not merely community refuse collecting services but also community house cleaning, rather like the present office cleaning firms; not just meals on wheels for the elderly, but for all dependents. But how far are these domestic roles to be taken over by the state and the community? That is an ideological issue.

Modern technology is commonly assumed to be fast freeing women from housework, and also shortening a man's working hours. This is certainly a common WL assumption, but a survey in France and another in America doubts the assumption except where a job is done outside the home, e.g. saving on sewing time once clothes are bought ready-made. But contrary to popular belief, washing machines etc. do not appear to have reduced a wife's time spent on household duties. It is, according to these findings, doubtful if domestic spare time is increasing due to technological advances. But when women do go out to work, does it decrease their domestic family life satisfaction? Negatively H. Feldman seeks to establish that, far from the arrival of baby bringing deep bliss, conjugal satisfaction begins to decrease when children arrive and is at its height when children have grown up and retirement comes. Kharchev and Golod argue that roughly half the Polish and Russian women who went out to work gave other than finance as their main motive, while an American survey suggests that only a small minority of working mothers are career orientated, and stress on self-assertion and self-realisation only tends to produce divorce. But young Czech professional women were found by J. Prokopec to have more social and intellectual ambition in jobs, quite apart from marriage aspirations. The overall sociological picture is far from coherent or complete, and a good deal of subjective assessment comes into sociological writing however subconsciously (it is not all subconscious, as the use of the words *myth* and *prejudice* in this book reveals). But even when the sociological facts are perfectly obtained, the ideological issue remains. In places the book does recognise that, especially when comparing the East European reactions with those in America.

With working mothers, whether full-time or part-time, there will always be a tension between job and family claims. (The problem exists for others too, e.g. the dedicated Christian who holds back from the missionfield to look after some relative, or the businessman who refrains from moving to a new job to be near an aged parent.) The Communist countries, who have much more large scale working married-woman-power than in the West, have never solved the basic tension as J. Piotrowski's account of the very mixed attitudes of Polish women makes clear. Where is the woman's prime loyalty? For the Christian we are back to the primary question of God's purpose in creation, *how*, and so far as we can ascertain *why*, he made the two sexes as he did. Modern technology has made some difference, and certainly contraception (and the more controversial abortion) has freed many women from unwanted pregnancies and unwanted children, but the ideological conflict remains. As Poloma and Garland conclude concerning American working mothers, 'Contrary to feminist writings, marriage and motherhood appears to be a great area of satisfaction for many professionally trained women. All but one of our respondents would not want to discontinue their professional activities, feeling that it added much to meet their own needs and thus contributed toward making their marriage a happier one' (p. 142). Perhaps there is some answer here to the churches' search for ways of using their professional womanpower—part-time jobs outside the home, with professional training and professional status, though that does not have to be ordination to the presbyterate. Part-time formally recognised church jobs might be at least part of a solution, but what would be quite deplorable would be any attempt to use women in church work as cheap labour. No one ever argues that, but it would be a bold man or woman who denied that it ever happened.

The right approach

IT is no part of our argument to suggest that those who want to ordain women subscribe to the philosophy of WL, but it is our conviction that very few Christians are fully aware of the background influence of the whole array of feminist thinking, nor are they aware of the real thrust of the most recent and militant form of feminism in WL, with its implications for drastic attacks on family life. Added to all this is a vague sense of unease that in church life somehow women have not of late quite had a fair chance. There is some danger therefore that such Christians may feel that to ordain women would be a suitable remedy, and that they will agree to this without asking the basic theological questions.

In chapter one of *Women & Holy Orders*, an official Church of England report, the first reason given under the chapter heading 'Why has the Question been reopened now?' was this:

> *The 'emancipation' of women*
> Women have now been accepted into almost every profession and taken their place competently alongside men. It is therefore understandable that the question should be raised whether women should be admitted also to Holy Orders.

We believe that this was a correct explanation of current church moods. It is true that the next paragraph says that those who are most ardently in favour of ordaining women regard this as only a minor argument, but then they are a small body of academics and 'advanced' churchmen with liberal theologies, and are certainly not representative of the average man in the pew, who is much more likely to think in terms of the quotation above.

Whether they are aware of it or not, feminist thinking is widespread today and has influenced churchmen. The next section in *Women & Holy Orders* is entitled 'The New Insights awakened by the spirit of the times'! We are not arguing here for or against particular feminist views (Hans Cavallin has done that), but we do want Christians to be aware of them in thinking out their answer to the matter of whether to ordain women. The crucial question is how we react to secular feminist pressure. One line of approach, and one which at times inevitably gets a lot of press coverage today, is to watch current trends in thought, and when they have become sufficiently powerful and influential, seek to accommodate Christianity to them and to attach something specifically Christian to the particular cause. There are plenty of examples of this today, as well as in church history: in theology, the accommodation of men like Rudolf Bultmann to the philosophy of secularists like Heidegger (see the dread consequences in a book like Joachim Kahl's atheistic *The Misery of Christianity*, 1971), or the succession of ecumenical crazes, such as theologies of revolution and ecclesiastical justification for draft dodging. Or go back to the interwar years: the idealistic pacifism, which now seems to have receded, or the attempt of the German Christians to christianise Nazism. Or go back further: the social gospel movement in America, or the radical evolutionist criticism of the Bible which prided itself on its objectivity and which is now seen to have been totally subjective. The characteristic of this approach is to spot current trends in thought, come to terms with them, and attempt to claim them as Christian. In stark contrast to this method stands the approach of Karl Barth who confronted every new idea and new situation with the Word of God, and judged it by that alone. Professor Otto Piper in his *Christian*

Ethics has an important section on the theological approach, culminating in this:
> Bringing the Bible up to date is an important and necessary task. But that goal will not be reached by ignoring the exegetical tradition of the past and reading modern problems into the text. Rather we shall be best served by relating our contemporary problems to the process of holy history as described and at work in the Bible.[13]

Barth and Piper are right. The Christian must sit under the Word of God in the Bible, be judged and directed by that rather than by current and passing fashions of thought and opinion, even if given a vaguely Christian veneer of respectability. There are constant dangers of slipping into the latter course as church history shows, but for those who take the Word as their foundation-stone there can be only one permissible approach. Sound theology must determine our thinking and our action as Christians.

Let us apply this to the ordination of women question. Take *Women & Holy Orders*, where the biblical evidence gets less than three of 134 pages (that in itself is significant for the report's approach, and indeed for current Anglican methodology). Gal. 3: 28 is rightly identified with baptism. 1 Cor. 11: 3-16: the argument is said only to concern covering the head. Doubts are raised about the authenticity of 1 Cor. 14: 34-35, and even if those verses are authentic, the discussion is said to be only about what is edifying. 1 Tim. 2: 12: the background is said to be uncertain, with the probability that the text is an antidote to some Gnostic error. The subordination texts in Paul are recognised, but it is asked if these texts apply outside marriage and if they are valid for all time. Paul is exonerated from antipathy to women in 1 Cor. 7, a view which is rightly exposed as a fallacy. The apostle is said to have taken contemporary views of women for granted, as anything else might have caused radical disruption at the time. The section ends thus: 'The theological question cannot be simply settled by a mechanical quoting of texts from scripture, the evidence of which has to be seen in its context and in relation to its total background.'

We regret that the Commission did not take its own advice. There is, alas, no attempt whatever to investigate the idea that Paul might be expounding part of God's revelation given to man at creation, though the Commission recognised the Genesis text at the back of all the Pauline texts (see their footnote). There is no attempt to find a biblical understanding of the male-female relationship which is basic to this question. Notice instead the constant hints at explaining away all awkward texts *ad hoc* as part of contemporary world views (the onus is on those who adopt such an approach to prove their case to the hilt, not assume their own hypotheses. All too often, consciously or unconsciously, that avenue becomes a convenient way of ditching what is out of harmony with current fashions, and here we are back to our basic approach question). Is Paul just a man of his time in accepting the Old Testament or is he an authoritative apostle submitting himself to the creation ordinances as revealed in Genesis, exactly as Jesus did over marriage? Was Jesus just accepting the limitations of his time, and if so, what are the christological implications of that?

Or take an acknowledged expert who shares this same deficient approach, Dr. D. Sherwin Bailey. It should be said that he is primarily an historian not a biblical scholar, but on p. 15 of *The Man-Woman Relation in Christian Thought* he writes:

> It is evident that the writers of the New Testament accepted without question the androcentric assumptions underlying the law and the social attitudes of Judaism and of the Graeco-Roman civilisation; and St. Paul even gave these assumptions a semblance of theological sanction by fitting the sexual relation into a universal hierarchial scale, according to which God, Christ, male, and female were set in a descending order of subordination. Woman, so the Scriptures declared, was created for the benefit of man, and must submit to him as her divinely appointed 'head': she was forbidden to teach in the church and was enjoined to keep silence, cultivating a meek and tranquil spirit, and learning 'in quietness with all subjection'; she was reminded, moreover, that Eve and not Adam was first beguiled into transgression—a stigma which long clung to her sex, branding every member of it as a 'weaker vessel', irresponsible, and a potential temptress.

Consider the implications and underlying assumptions in that quote. Paul just accepted current ideas, and even gave them theological sanctions (an exact description of the method we are contesting!). The implication is that Paul is rather unfortunate by modern standards in what he said. But where is the writer's doctrine of revelation? By what criterion does he sort out what are ancient views and what eternal truth, and was Christ limited in just the same way as Paul? It does not seem to have occurred to Bailey here that God might have planned his universe and the whole male-female relationship in that hierarchical way. Contrast this with Professor Otto Piper's exposition of a total biblical view of male-female relationships.[14] Piper shows how biblical ideas contrast strongly with mere biological or humanistic views of male-female relationships:

> The second account of the creation of man in Gen. 2: 7 is in its present context meant to serve as a commentary on the first one (Gen. 1: 23-30) by stressing the difference of the sexes. Accordingly, woman's legal status among the Hebrews was quite different from that of the man. The Bible attaches such importance to the differentiation of the sexes that the full destination of man cannot be obtained except by means of it.

Piper's excellent discussion is too long to cite in full, but a few short extracts must suffice:

> Rejecting all attempts to ascribe the husband's superiority to any natural male qualities, Paul reminds the Corinthians that the man holds this position by divine appointment, and the man's inability to reproduce himself is a clear indication that by God's will a definite limitation has been imposed on the natural state of masculinity (1 Cor. 11: 11-12).

Unless we realise that the relationship of the sexes is determined by God's plan for mankind it must seem objectionable to modern people that the woman is told to 'fear' her husband (Eph. 5: 33) and to be subject and obedient to him (1 Pet. 3: 1; 1 Cor. 14: 34). These demands are not the remnants of an obsolete social order of antiquity but rather derive from the fact that God contrived to redeem mankind by a man rather than by a woman.

Man's superiority* is derived from the fact that the woman was created out of man and for him, but not vice versa (1 Cor. 11: 8 cf. 1 Tim 2: 13). Besides, in Christ's being the Head of the Church, Paul finds a revelation of the true meaning of the sexual relationship (1 Cor. 11: 3). In other words, the superiority of the man, and thus the subjection of the woman, is a fundamental phenomenon of human life. That this mutual relation should often cause pain and displeasure in married life is not due to man's position of lordship but rather to the fact that sinful men and women are not willing to accord loving consideration to their partner's interest.

C. S. Lewis sees the point in his usual perceptive way. Writing of the male imagery of God, and answering the question of whether, if God is without sex, we cannot turn all masculine descriptions of God into the feminine, he says:[15]

> But Christians think that God himself has taught us how to speak of him. To say that it does not matter is to say either that all the masculine imagery is not inspired, is merely human in origin, or else that, though inspired, it is quite arbitrary and unessential. And this is surely intolerable: or, if tolerable, it is an argument not in favour of Christian priestesses, but against Christianity.

Lewis saw the importance of taking God's revelation at its face value.

We cannot underline too strongly the importance of asking the basic question and in the right form. What does the Bible say about the

---

*Whatever phraseology is used to expound this biblical idea, it is important to realise that such writers are trying to explain the notion of a hierarchical order which God placed in society, as stated in Genesis and expounded later by Paul. Piper writes of 'superiority', but he is careful to point out that this is not some essential male superiority, but a difference of created order. Bishop K. E. Kirk writing primarily of married relationships insists, 'The subordination of woman to man in the full sex-relation is a subordination of *function*, not of *essential nature*' (*Beauty and Bands*, p. 183). Bishop Hensley Henson argues, 'The only equality of the sexes which the Church can rightly make the basis of its practical system recognises difference of natural function and accepts the principle of subordination in common service. Sex is a factor of such importance that any attempt to ignore it in the sphere of ecclesiastical order must defeat itself. Only by frankly admitting difference can genuine equality be secured. Subordination is the very principle of ordered society, and it has its first expression and ultimate sanction in the Home' (*Bishoprick Papers*, p. 10). It is interesting to note that here we have three theologians writing out of very different traditions (an Evangelical Lutheran, a very Broad Liberal Anglican and an Anglican Catholic), and yet they all come to the same conclusion. Cf. also V. A. Demant's survey of the differences between the sexes in *Women & Holy Orders*, pp. 105-8. The biblical principle of hierarchy and subordination is not to be thought of in terms of preserving outmoded male superiority as feminists are apt to assume. It is certainly no cringing servility, but rather an attempt to explain what the Bible means by dependence, and is ultimately true femininity.

whole range of male-female relationships, and what bearing does that have on the possibility of ordaining women? It is not the task of the church to accept current fashions uncritically, and vaguely christianise them, but to confront them with and test them by the Word of God. If the case for ordaining women can be made out from the Bible, or even if it can be clearly demonstrated that there is nothing in the Bible against it, then it is at least an open question; but those are the tests, and it is not enough to explain away all biblical texts *ad hoc* and then imagine that there are no theological objections.[16] There is no virtue in defending tradition for tradition's sake, though if a Christian tradition has persisted for centuries, it ought to make a responsible Christian pause and ask what lies behind it. But equally there is no virtue, rather the reverse, in Christians giving in to prevalent feminist thinking if it is in conflict with biblical theology.

Male and female in the Creator's plan

ONCE the determination to take the *whole* biblical teaching seriously, as Piper and Lewis insist, is adopted, the question of ordination of women to the ministry of the church is seen to be part of the wider issue of the way God has made men and women, and how together they fit into his divine plan for mankind. There is an urgent need here for a detailed study by a theologian who is capable of seeing biblical theology as a whole. Those who write off Old Testament ideas as if they were merely the conventions of antiquity will never arrive at a balanced answer. The whole role of man and woman, and indeed of the basic family unit within society, needs to be re-examined in the light of WL and other current challenges. Such a study would need to cover the role of the family in God's plan, the role of single men and women outside marriage, and God's very purpose for community life in creation.

Despite avant garde notions of communes and the kibbutz, there is no evidence that any sizeable group in western society wants to abandon the family unit as the basis of civilised society (the Communists tried it in Russia after the Revolution but soon went back on that idea). Yet the family concept is under increasing attack both directly and indirectly, *directly* from revolutionaries like the WL, and *indirectly* through permissive sexual morality and situation ethics, through the image of sex presented by advertising and the media, and through pornography and obscenity.

What does feminism say about biblical ideas? Recent WL writers usually ignore them. Juliet Mitchell dismisses Paul with contempt;[17] Kate Millett only discusses them incidentally in her historical and literary survey. Eva Figes has a chapter entitled 'A Man's God', but it can hardly be taken seriously as theology.[18] It starts with Genesis, goes off into obscurity about ancient Near Eastern legends and primitive savages, barely glances at Paul, and then jumps to Augustine. That is Miss Figes' professional journalism, not theology. The more restrained academic approach of Dr. Rover provides the answer. At the end of a chapter entitled 'Introduction to *The Enemy*' she says:[19]

> The battle goes on; the support given by religion to the conventional roles of the sexes has diminished along with the decline in religious belief, but to some extent its place has been taken by Freudian ideas supporting (or thought to be supporting) the thesis that women find fulfilment only as wives and mothers.

It seems the WL revolutionaries do not think the churches worth bothering about any more. Instead they have turned on Freud and others. Juliet Mitchell's chapter 'The Ideology of the Family' is not interested in religion (or Freud) but discusses the whole thing in terms of left-wing economic and social theory. Kate Millett rounds on such 'progressive' writers as Lawrence for his 'cunning sabotage of the feminist argument' and Miller for his 'flamboyant contempt for it'.[20]

In early American feminism there was an attempt to give feminism a Christian veneer, as the early documents in O'Neill's book show, but when analysed it is not a coherent theological argument, only a veneer of Christian phraseology. Not surprisingly it soon disappeared, being replaced by secularist egalitarianism such as occurs in Wollstonecraft and Mill. Is the basic appeal of motherhood and family life for the vast majority of women (even in modern urbanised society) dying? It is interesting to note that when in the '30s the Nazis wanted to break up German feminism, which was at the time well led by Gertrud Bäumer, well organised and well established, they could not do it through Nazi women, as the party hardly contained any. They succeeded by an appeal to family life in the home and by contrasting this with the intellectual ideals of feminism, pacifism, humanitarianism, etc. in the older leaders. They would not have succeeded if the appeal of the home had not been so strong.[21]

Christians should appreciate that attacks, whatever their origin, on the family concept are onslaughts on the very foundations of Christian society. It is important for Christians to ask if the hierarchical structure of family life is part of the divinely revealed plan, part of the way God made men and women, the way we observe their make up in everyday life, and if so, whether this concept is compatible with feminist egalitarianism. To speak of the 'equality' of women with men sounds superficially very moral and Christian, but interpreted so as to conflict with the divine plan for male-female relationships, it may prove unchristian, indeed antichristian. The concept of 'equality' of the sexes is in danger of destroying women's femininity and reducing them to mere substitute males. Such a concept wants very close examination before Christians accept it.

Lay ministry in the churches

THE third argument for reopening the question of ordaining women in *Women & Holy Orders* was 'The failure of the Church to provide an adequate ministry for women'. The paragraph following rightly sees this question as part of the whole problem of the ministry of the laity, but that important point is often overlooked. The details obviously vary from church to church, but there is a general bewilderment in practice about lay ministry, much talk, we suspect, but little real action. For instance Methodists, who had a great tradition of lay preachers, in the past a real source of strength, now report, in Britain at any rate, a sad decline. Presbyterians who for years have had a tradition of lay elders seem, according to a comment from a Presbyterian theologian friend, to have very few laity in positions of real responsibility, and he writes from the heart of Presbyterianism in Scotland. The Church of England has for some years possessed lay readers, with their theological dichotomy between word and sacrament, but Ecclesia Anglicana still retains the centuries old tradition of clerical domination in its local church leadership. Reading the odd lesson, taking a collection, or even being a churchwarden are no solutions to an adequate lay ministry, and the recent tendency to make women lay readers exactly as male lay readers merely confuses things further. What is needed, certainly in the Church of England, is an overall re-examination of the whole structure of ministry, into which male and female, lay and ordained, all can fit in the light of a sound theology. Ministry of women in the widest sense, not just ordination to the presbyterate, has to be seen in this larger context of ministry as a whole, for even if women were to be ordained to the presbyterate, that would affect only very few persons, and it would still do hardly anything to alleviate the current unease about the whole place in the church of lay women with obvious gifts.

NOTES

[1] D. S. Bailey, *The Man-Woman Relation in Christian Thought*, 1959, p. 14. Juliet Mitchell, *Woman's Estate*, 1971, p. 112. K. Hudson, *Men & Women*, 1968, p. 21. E. Figes, *Patriarchal Attitudes*, 1970, ch. 2. C. Rover, *Love, Morals & Feminists*, 1970, p. 4, though more guardedly.
[2] *Women*, 1970, p. 31.
[3] W. L. O'Neill, *The Woman Movement*, 1969, p. 111.
[4] p. 93, and Rover, p. 154.
[5] Mitchell, p. 11.
[6] p. 13.
[7] p. 19.
[8] Bryan Wilson, *Youth Culture & the Universities*.
[9] pp. 76ff.
[10] pp. 99, 105, 108.
[11] S. Firestone, *The Dialectic of Sex*, 1971, pp. 233-237.
[12] Edited by A. Michel, Brill, Leiden, 1971. The discussion in the rest of this section centres round this symposium. The reader should examine the detailed evidence in the book.

[13] *Christian Ethics*, 1970, pp. 123ff.
[14] O. A. Piper, *The Biblical View of Sex & Marriage*, 1960, ch. 11, pp. 90ff.
[15] C. S. Lewis, *Undeceptions*, 1971, p. 194.
[16] O. Jessie Lace in *The Ordination of Women to the Historic Ministry of the Church* does exactly this: 'In the twentieth century we can only regard Gen. 2 as an interesting example of this kind [patriarchal society] of story and profitable for purposes of comparison only' (p. 3), and 1 Tim. 2: 15 'is wholly incompatible with the understanding of salvation in the rest of the New Testament' (p. 5). Such arbitrary dismissal of difficult passages simply will not do. Marga Bührig hints, though more guardedly, in the same direction 'The NT, like the OT, was of course written in a society based on a patriarchal structure, and this structure is presupposed in its text. But it is no more binding on us than is the conception of the world we encounter in the creation accounts' (*Technology & Social Justice*, ed. R. H. Preston, p. 316).
[17] p. 112.
[18] Figes, ch. 2.
[19] Rover, p. 6.
[20] Millett, p. 362.
[21] C. Kirkpatrick, *Woman in Nazi Germany*, 1939, ch. 2.

Books on Feminism

WE believe it unlikely that many Christians will be acquainted with the detailed history and arguments of feminism, and with the advent of WL it is all but impossible to keep abreast of the publications, and any list is liable to be out of date before it is printed. Nevertheless the following guide (to the end of 1971) may be useful: Juliet Mitchell's *Woman's Estate* contains a popular account of the history and programme of WL. Kate Millett's *Sexual Politics* comes from America, is marked on the jacket 'World bestseller' and aims to show anti-feminist bias in culture between 1830 and 1920; it is a serious academic book. Shulamith Firestone's *The Dialectic of Sex* is the fullest case yet for the feminist revolution, marked by youthful passion rather than detailed documentation. Kenneth Hudson's *Men & Women* and Eva Figes' *Patriarchal Attitudes* are both lightweight and journalistic impressions. *Woman in Nazi Germany* by C. Kirkpatrick is a detailed specialist study; it is important when assessing feminist manifestoes to know exactly what left and right wing regimes have done in the recent past. Katharine Moore's *Women* is a popular but very readable account of women through the ages. Easily the best historical books, both by qualified academics, are Constance Rover's *Love, Morals & the Feminists* (plus her earlier works on Women's Suffrage and J. S. Mill and Harriet Taylor) for the English side, and Professor W. L. O'Neill's *The Woman Movement* for the US side and a comparison with England. His book contains selected documents. *Woman on Woman* by M. Laing contains a vigorous selection of feminist polemic, full of sex and baby problems; but with one significantly milder chapter—by a nun.

The Office of Woman in the Church, to the Present Day

R. T. BECKWITH

VARIOUS INFLUENCES are discernible in the history of woman's ministry in the Christian Church. Some of these influences are manifestly biblical, while others are secular. Even when the Church has been most concerned to implement biblical teaching, it has not been uninfluenced, in its interpretation of that teaching, by the customs and ideas current in contemporary society; and the fact that biblical teaching itself has a social background, which makes it necessary to distinguish between principles and their application, should not be ignored, as it often has been. It would be a mistake, however, to think that the history of woman's ministry, since it reflects a degraded idea of womanhood which is now outgrown, has no lessons (except warnings) for the Church of today. For the truth is that degraded ideas of womanhood are not confined to the past, and exalted ideas of womanhood are not confined to the present. In fact, as Canon Demant writes,

There is no general advance in the position of women as time goes on. Many primitive cultures are matriarchal and their return is sighed for by some people today.[1] In the ancient western world scholars find societies where women were held in high regard, where they had liberties and dominant influence.[2] In many periods and regions in the Middle Ages women's position was a strong one. They could influence secular society from their personal positions and from their official ones in the religious orders. Medieval popular literature, like that of the eighteenth and nineteenth centuries, is spiced with tales of men being bullied by their wives. Many Renaissance women won great esteem for their learning and leadership. And all this without any movement for women's rights. The denigration of women is not an age-long habit which has lately been cured by historical advance. Some of the most vicious and derogatory views on women were expressed as late as the last century and this. Schopenhauer, Kierkegaard, Strindberg regarded women as inferior creatures. Ibsen depicted them as such even with his theoretical belief in their emancipation. P. J. Mobius wrote of *The Psychological Debility of Women* as if they were entirely moved by instinct. Otto Weininger in *Sex and Character* (1926) appealed to Immanuel Kant for support in his polemic that woman is infrapersonal. And all this in an age also influenced by J. S. Mill's *The Subjection of Women*! The conclusion is that recognition of women's powers, abilities and influence is not the result of a historical progressive movement but comes and goes with certain cultures and attitudes.³

We shall therefore proceed to trace the ways in which the different strands of biblical teaching relating to the ministry of women have been developed in Church history, noting as we do so the colouring which this teaching has received from the cultural circumstances of the Church.

The Married Life

BOTH in the Old Testament and in the New, the married state is one of great dignity. According to the Old Testament, the purpose of woman's creation was that she should be the married helpmate of man (Gen. 2: 18-24): thus her vocation is all one with her husband's. It is not until we reach the New Testament that any explicit attention is given to the single state. In the New Testament the married state is likewise normal, even in those writings where ascetic ideals are held forth. Thus, in the First Epistle to Timothy, insistence on celibacy is condemned as a doctrine of demons (4: 1-3), widows under sixty years of age are bidden to remarry (5: 14), and the way of salvation for a woman is stated to be not as a pastor and teacher but as a wife and mother (2: 11-15). Elsewhere in the New Testament the honour due to marriage is both directly asserted (Heb. 13: 4) and magnificently illustrated (Eph. 5: 21-33). The wife and mother, though subordinate to her husband, is herself assigned a position of great dignity by both Testaments. She orders and governs her household (Prov. 31: 10-31; 1 Tim. 5: 14) and receives honour and obedience from her children (Ex. 20: 12; Dt. 27: 16; Prov. 30: 17; Matt. 15: 3-9; Eph. 6: 1-3; Col. 3: 20).

As in the Bible, so in the history of the Church, the normal role of woman has been as wife and mother, and her normal sphere the home. Even those women who have not married have very often devoted themselves to domestic duties. This does not mean that, whether married or unmarried, they have had time for nothing else. The spare-time service of married women has the encouragement of the New Testament, whether it takes the form of witness (Jn. 4: 28-29, 39-42; Acts 18: 26) or of ministration to bodily needs (1 Tim. 5: 10), and an impressive survey of the voluntary work (evangelistic, educational and social) which has been developed in the Church since the nineteenth century is given by Kathleen Bliss in chapter 2 of her valuable book *The Service and Status of Women in the Churches* (London, SCM, 1952). Nevertheless, the bearing and early nurture of children is itself a very demanding responsibility, as is the supervision and care of a home, and the latter also falls mainly upon the wife because the husband is preoccupied with earning their living. The vocation of wife and mother has always been respected by Christians, but especially since the Reformation and in the reformed Churches, as the excessive emphasis which from the third century onwards was placed upon the celibate calling led to a certain disparagement of marriage, and to restrictions upon it, against which the sixteenth century Reformers strongly reacted.

It ought to be mentioned in this connection that some married women have played a very important part in Christian history through the eminence of their husbands and sons. Both in the East and in the West the wives and mothers of kings and emperors have had a crucial share in the extension of Christianity—among others, Helena, the mother of the Emperor Constantine; Olga, the grandmother of Prince Vladimir of Kiev, the 'apostle of Russia'; Clothilde, the wife of King Clovis of the Franks; and, in England, Bertha, the wife of King Ethelbert of Kent.

Similarly, in those ages and areas of Christendom which have encouraged clerical marriage, the wives of the clergy have, because of their husbands' office, played a unique part in the forwarding of the Church's work. They have taken responsibility for the duty of clerical hospitality (1 Tim. 3: 2; Tit. 1: 8), and have been their husbands' closest counsellors and partners in work among women, children and families.

The Ministry of the Widow

BOTH the Old Testament and the New show a tender concern for the affliction and destitution of the wife who has lost her husband and the child who has lost his father (Is. 1: 17; Jas. 1: 27). He who oppresses them in their reduced and defenceless condition offends most heinously against God (Dt. 27: 19; Mk. 12: 40) who is their defender and vindicator (Ex. 22: 22-24; Ps. 68: 5; 146: 9; Is. 10: 1-4). In the earliest days of the Church, we find their poverty being relieved by other Christians (Acts 6: 1; 9: 36-41), and in the fifth chapter of the First Epistle to Timothy we find aged widows being enrolled for such relief. The directions there given are that only those who are without children or grandchildren to relieve them shall be enrolled (vv. 3-8), and only those who have reached sixty years of age (vv. 9, 11, 14), below which age they can provide for themselves or remarry (vv. 11-15; cf. 1 Cor. 7: 9, 39). Another condition is that they should have lived good Christian lives and ministered to the needs of others (vv. 9-10). Though their enrolment (v. 9) is, in context, primarily for relief, it is also a consecration to Christ, excluding subsequent remarriage (vv. 11-12; cf. 1 Cor. 7: 8, 34, 40); but remarriage earlier is apparently not excluded (v. 14), provided it was not in their first husband's lifetime (v. 9). Nothing is explicitly said about their way of life after enrolment: their prayers (v. 5) are the natural consequence of their destitution, their upbringing of their children (v. 10) evidently refers to an earlier period of their life, and their ministry to the needs of others (*ibid.*) would be most practicable before they became destitute. The danger of idleness (v. 13) suggests that they have no specific duties. Nevertheless, they would not be expected to desist from prayer after enrolment, nor (except in as far as their circumstances required) from beneficence.

From these tenuous beginnings, the early Church developed its famous order of widows.[4] The earliest clear references to this order are in the writings of Clement of Alexandria (*Pedagogue* 3: 12), Tertullian (*Veiling of Virgins* 9, *Monogamy* 11) and Hippolytus (*Apostolic Tradition* 11) about the beginning of the third century, but it is frequently referred to after this, in the documents known as Church Orders and elsewhere. How far the order was a new creation, based on the patristic interpretation of Scripture, and how far it was a development of traditional practice, one can only speculate. The directions given in the *Apostolic Tradition* and in the third century *Didascalia* (chs. 14, 15, 18) are mainly based on 1 Tim. 5, and it is noteworthy that there the office of the widow is stated to be not teaching, baptising or celebrating the eucharist, but praying. This is a function common to all Christians, Hippolytus points out, and the widow is therefore not to be ordained. In the *Didascalia* she is instructed to stay at home, and, apart from praying, is encouraged to work with her hands for the benefit of others. She is only to go abroad at the bidding of the bishops and deacons, for example to pray over the sick, with fasting and the laying on of hands. The teaching of the *Apostolic Constitutions* in the following century is very much the same (bk. 3, paras. 1-15), and there once more it is explicitly stated that a widow is not ordained (bk. 8, para. 25). On the other hand, Clement of Alexandria, Tertullian and others list widows with bishops, priests and deacons as belonging to the clergy. The order of widows began to decline in the third century and disappeared about the end of the fourth, being replaced by the order of deaconesses, who could be widows, though normally virgins.

Another opening which at this juncture began to be supplied for widows, and for their traditional ministry of prayer and good works, was the life of the convent. At certain periods, large numbers of widows have devoted themselves to monasticism, for example in the Slavonic countries and Rumania during the Mongol occupation. Thus Militsa, widow of the last Serbian ruler Lazar (1371-89), founded a convent for the widows of the slain and became their abbess.

In modern times, a new task has developed in some parts of the world for the woman whom advancing years and bereavement have released from the more onerous of her domestic cares. In most heathen countries where Christian missions are at work, the task of Biblewoman has hitherto fallen almost exclusively to widows. In these cultures, only the widow is free to minister to her fellow-countrywomen and their families in this way, and is acceptable in doing so.[5]

The Ascetic Vocation

SIDE by side with the married life, the New Testament sets out a vocation to celibacy on which the Old Testament is silent. We have already noticed that the enrolled widow is not to remarry, but the vocation to the single life is by no means confined to the enrolled widow. It extends to other classes of widows and to the unmarried, but only to those among them 'to whom it is given' (Matt. 19: 11; 1 Cor. 7: 7). Those who can receive the calling to celibacy should (Matt. 19: 12; 1 Cor. 7: 7-9, 38, 40), because the married are more vulnerable to tribulations (1 Cor. 7: 26-28; cf. Mk. 13: 17), because the Christian should cultivate a spirit of detachment from the circumstances of this life, including marriage (1 Cor. 7: 29-31; cf. Lk. 20: 27-36), and because it is easier for the unmarried to attend upon the Lord without distraction (1 Cor. 7: 32-35; cf. Matt. 19: 12). The effect that this teaching has had upon the history of the Christian Church, accentuated as it has been by ascetic influences from outside, could hardly be exaggerated.

From the beginning of Christian literature, evidence appears of men and women who deliberately followed the celibate vocation (Ignatius, *To Polycarp* 5; Athenagoras, *Embassy* 33), and with the coming of the third century we find separate attention being devoted to the case of virgins (Tertullian, *Veiling of Virgins*; Hippolytus, *Apostolic Tradition* 13; Cyprian, *Dress of Virgins, Epistle 61*). Ignatius allows them to make their vocation known to the bishop, and Hippolytus rules that they are not part of the ordained ministry, which shows the public character that they have by his time acquired in the Church. In the fourth century, Basil (*Epistle 199*) and Cyril of Jerusalem (*Catechetical Lectures* 4: 24) speak of them as an 'order', and they appear from the account of the historian Socrates (*Ecclesiastical History* 1: 17) to have been enrolled in a register and to be the recipients of public generosity. In the same century, the *Apostolic Constitutions* appoint for them a share of tithe (bk. 2, para 25; bk. 8, para. 30), so that they may have ' leisure for piety ' (bk. 8, para. 24). In this period, poverty was no necessary part of their vocation[6], and they lived not in communities but at home.[7]

Since virgins were allowed to make their profession at an early age, this situation involved the same perils which St. Paul foresaw would result if the younger widows were enrolled (1 Tim. 5: 11-13), and in the present case the perils became sad realities, as the writings of Cyprian, Basil and Ambrose (*The Virgin's Fall*) attest. Cyprian's remedy was to allow those who could not persevere to marry (*Epistle 61*). This, however, would not avoid the scandal of the broken profession, the root cause of which was the publicity now attached to the celibate vocation. The remedy generally adopted, however, was not to permit marriage or to make the celibate vocation a purely personal and private matter, but to treat those who lapsed with a severity which must have been a contributory cause to their withdrawal from the society of the other sex into convents. Basil and Ambrose both counsel severity, and the sixteenth canon of the Council of Chalcedon (AD 451) gave it legislative sanction.

The gathering of professed celibates into monasteries and convents began in the fourth century, and in time obliterated the earlier system.[8] It was at this point that the other two elements in the monastic ideal, voluntary poverty and obedience to a superior, became associated with the celibate vocation. Voluntary poverty, like celibacy, has its roots in the New Testament, where we find not only grave warnings against the love of riches and moving exhortations to generosity addressed to all Christians, but a call to poverty addressed to the disciples and apostles (Lk. 12: 33; 2 Cor. 6: 10) and to those who are ensnared by wealth (Matt. 19: 16-30; cf. Mk. 9: 43-48). In the New Testament, however, the calling to celibacy and the calling to poverty have no necessary connection. Obedience to a superior has precedents in the New Testament, where submission and obedience in the home, in the congregation and in the state are basic principles of Christian living, but it is there balanced by stress on the individual's direct responsibility to Christ and to God, which takes precedence over all other relationships (Matt. 10: 34-37; Mk. 3: 21, 31-35; Acts 4: 19; 5: 29). In practice, the individual poverty of the monk or nun only too easily became the corporate wealth and luxury of the community to which he belonged, and the severance of one group of human relationships became the establishment of a new group of human relationships, even more inimical to a single-minded attendance upon the Lord.[9]

Nevertheless, the old idealism survived. As has rightly been said,

> All down the centuries the line of women 'religious' runs parallel with that of hermits, monks, friars and founders, the one complementary to the other. Far back in the age of the desert fathers, Pachomius was building a convent for his sister Mary. There were Basil and Macrina, Ambrose and Marcellina his sister, for whom he wrote his treatise on virginity, Augustine and Felicitas—his letters for her guidance in the government of her Community form the basis of the Augustinian Rule. There were Benedict and Scholastica, Francis and Clare, John of the Cross and Teresa, Francis de Sales and Jane Chantal, Vincent de Paul and Louise de Marillac, whose Sisters of Charity, founded in the seventeenth century, were the first Order of women to be unenclosed and given over to the care of the sick and poor.[10]

The monastic life flourishes in the Church of Rome to this day, and, in a reduced condition, has continued in the East; and the good it has done, in evangelism, in education, in nursing, in hospitality to strangers and care of the deprived, and in keeping before the Church a high ideal of Christian dedication, is immense.

In the reformed Churches, monasticism came almost to a complete end in the sixteenth century. This was due partly to the contemporary corruption of monastic life, which lay not so much in excesses of asceticism as in luxury and idleness, but partly to more basic causes. The great Reformers (whatever may be true of their successors) were no enemies to the celibate vocation. They were, however, enemies to binding vows of celibacy, which they regarded as a perilous snare; to the seclusion which accompanied these vows (except among the secular clergy, whose immorality was a parallel evil); and to the denigration of marriage by which these vows were justified. They rejected the hoary distinction between precepts of obligation and counsels of perfection, pointing out that 'each man has his own gift from God, one after this manner, and another after that' (1 Cor. 7: 7), and that marriage is therefore not just a permissible vocation but the highest vocation for the man who is called to it. In the few convents which survived the Reformation, consequently, as a few did among the Lutherans in Germany and Denmark, the binding vows were abolished. One of these convents, the Augustinian nunnery of St. Marienberg in Helmstedt, has continued to the present day, and some new Lutheran and Presbyterian convents have been founded in this century. The Sisterhood of Mary at Darmstadt may be instanced, and the Iona community, which is a semi-monastic community of men and women in the Church of Scotland. Anglican convents, of the traditional type, were revived in 1845 under the influence of the Oxford Movement, and have since become quite numerous. If, however, the monastic life is really to flourish in the Churches of the Reformation, serious account will have to be taken of the theological critique which the Reformers levelled at unreformed monasticism, and the three ideals of chastity, poverty and obedience will need to be carefully re-examined, both individually and in their relationship with each other.

The Office of Deaconess

IN Rom. 16: 1-2, St. Paul commends to the Roman Church 'Phoebe our sister, being a *diakonos* of the church that is at Cenchreae . . . that ye assist her in whatsoever matter she may have need of you, for she herself also hath been a succourer of many, and of mine own self'. Dr. Blum has argued that the participle before *diakonos*, and the genitive case following it, imply that it is a technical term and should be translated '*deaconess*'. If this is so, it lends support to the belief (which Dr. Blum does not, however, share) that in a later epistle Paul is again referring to deaconesses. This is in 1 Tim. 3: 11, where the subject is qualifications for the diaconate, and the statement is made: 'Women in like manner must be grave, not slanderers, temperate, faithful in all things'. The arguments against identifying the 'women' here with deacons' wives are that the Greek word has no article, and that nothing is said in the preceding verses about the qualities needed in the wives of bishops. This suggests that Chrysostom, and most modern commentators with him, are right in understanding the 'women' to be female deacons. Nevertheless, the question cannot be considered as closed, and the ambiguous status of deaconesses both in the ancient world and in modern times must be partly attributed to legitimate doubt whether they are in fact female deacons or not.

The functions of the deaconess in New Testament times can only be inferred. The help that Phoebe might require from the Roman Church was no doubt mainly material, and since the apostle draws a parallel between this help and the help that Phoebe had given to himself and others, it has been supposed that she was a woman of means. It is no objection to this that she was a female deacon, for it must be insisted that the diaconate was an office of considerable dignity, as is not only stated in 1 Tim. 3: 13, but is implied by the fact that in 1 Tim. 3 and Phil. 1: 1 the deacons are closely linked with the presbyter-bishops, and these two offices alone are singled out from all the ministries of Christians for special attention. The deacons should probably be viewed as assistants to the presbyter-bishops. There is, however, a possible objection to the belief that Phoebe was a woman of means in the fact that in this case she would hardly have needed material help from the Roman Church. It seems more likely, therefore, that the help which she gave to St. Paul and others she gave in her capacity as deaconess, and not as woman of means, and consequently that she gave it not out of her own resources but out of the resources of the church at Cenchreae.

Apart from ministering to material needs, the deaconess would doubtless share in the other assistant functions of the male deacon. These would not in the apostolic period include teaching the congregation (1 Cor. 14: 33-36; 1 Tim. 2: 12-15), but it is noteworthy that in 1 Tim. 3 aptness to teach is not required of the male deacon either, as it is of the bishop (v. 2; cf. Tit. 1: 9). From the position in which the reference to deaconesses is inserted in 1 Tim. 3, it may be inferred that what follows does not apply to them and that they would not normally be married, no doubt because motherhood and the care of a home would make it difficult for them to fulfil their diaconate. Nevertheless, there is certainly no prohibition of marriage here, as there is in the case of the enrolled widow.

The next reference to deaconesses comes early in the second century, in Pliny's *Letter 96, To Trajan*.[11] The letter is written in Latin, and he refers to those in the Christian congregation who are called *ministrae*. There is then silence about deaconesses until the third century *Didascalia* (ch. 16). The order of widows had come to prominence in the meantime, and since the silence of a writer who gives so full an account of the various orders in the Church as Tertullian cannot be accidental, any more than that of a writer who treats them so systematically as Hippolytus, it seems likely that widows for a time did duty for deaconesses. The order of widows began to decline in the third century, as we have seen, but the *Didascalia* and the later Church Orders show the two offices co-existing for a time, the deaconess sometimes taking the pre-eminence (as in the *Apostolic Constitutions*) and the widow at other times (as in the *Testamentum Domini*). In the *Didascalia* the deaconess is a female deacon, and like the male deacon is a personal assistant to the bishop. She assists at the baptism of women, for modesty's sake, but may not herself baptise (which, at the bishop's bidding, the deacon may do). She also instructs the newly baptised women. She visits women in their houses (which, if they have heathen husbands, a deacon could not do without arousing suspicions), ministers to them when they are sick or infirm, and informs the bishop of any who are indigent. Additional duties mentioned in documents written a century or so later are keeping the doors at which women enter church and supervising them in their places (*Apostolic Constitutions* 2: 57; 8: 28) and taking the eucharist to them in their homes when they are sick (*Testamentum Domini* 2: 20). In the East between the fourth and ninth centuries some deaconesses were eminent teachers,[12] and they were sometimes appointed to be superiors of convents.

According to the *Apostolic Constitutions*, deaconesses are to be chosen from among those who are virgins or at least from once-married widows (bk. 6, para. 17). They are to be ordained by the laying on of the bishop's hands (bk. 8, paras. 19-20). Like the widows and virgins, they have a share of tithe for their maintenance (bk. 2, para. 25; bk. 8, para. 30). In the following century, the fifteenth canon of the Council of Chalcedon likewise rules that they are to be ordained, and are not to marry after ordination. The minimum age that it fixes for their ordination is forty.[13] On the other hand, ordination was not favoured in the West, and several Gallican synods of the fifth and sixth centuries forbade them to be ordained.

It will be obvious from all that we have said that there was a good deal of assimilation between widow, virgin and deaconess; and just as the widow at one time did duty for the deaconess, so after the disappearance of the order of widows about the end of the fourth century the deaconess did duty for the widow; similarly, when the order of deaconesses itself disappeared, about the tenth century in the West and about two centuries later in the East, the nun did duty for both. The disappearance of the deaconess has been attributed to the decline in the number of adult baptisms, but other factors may well have been the magnetism of the convent and the development (from the fourth century onwards) of the conception of the diaconate as a first step to the priesthood.

The revival of the office of deaconess is an achievement of the reformed Churches, and effectively dates from 1836, when the Lutheran pastor Theodor Fliedner founded a Deaconess Institute in his parish of Kaiserswerth.[14] Fliedner's deaconess was suggested by the ancient orders of deaconess and widow, but was more than a little influenced by the Sisters of Charity in the Church of Rome. The influence of monasticism is evident in the fact that the continental deaconess practices the monastic ideals of poverty, chastity and obedience, though without vows, that she wears a habit, and that much of her work has always been done in communities, which serve both as training centres and as hospitals. All the same, the majority of deaconesses are attached to parishes, and they may marry, though by doing so they cease to be deaconesses. Many also go out as foreign missionaries. Their primary work is pastoral, but they are not ordained, as is natural in Churches which do not ordain deacons either.

From Germany, the deaconess movement rapidly spread to other countries, supplying as it did a new outlet for the energies of dedicated women without domestic responsibilities, such as had not been open to them between the sixteenth and the nineteenth centuries. Deaconesses are now to be found in many different countries and denominations, and it is noteworthy that the order has recently been revived by the Orthodox Church in Greece. In England, the office developed side by side with other new ministries, such as those of the Salvation Army officer and Church Army sister, the lay parish worker, the Church social worker and the woman missionary. Single women had begun to be sent out as missionaries about 1827, when Mary Newell was sent to Malacca by the London Missionary Society. On the mission fields, women often had exceptional scope for their ministry, owing to the dearth of male missionaries. Other ministries for women which have now developed are those of directors of religious education, trained youth leaders, Sunday School organisers, chaplains' assistants (as in hospitals, prisons, universities and the armed forces), lay workers attached not to a parish but to a deanery or a team ministry, and teachers of theology.[15] Many of the Free Churches have female lay preachers, and the Church of England recently decided that women should be admitted to the corresponding auxiliary office, that of lay reader.

In the Church of England, the first deaconess to be authorised by a bishop was Elizabeth Ferard, set apart by the Bishop of London in 1862. From England the movement spread to other parts of the Anglican Communion, and in 1889 the Protestant Episcopal Church in the USA passed a canon giving the deaconess a degree of recognition which she had still not attained in England. Even this canon left many questions unanswered, and in January 1899 Bishop William Collins of Gibraltar published an influential article in the *Church Quarterly Review*, which was later reprinted as Appendix 7 to the 1919 report on *The Ministry of Women*, pointing out the serious ambiguities surrounding this office. Was the deaconess allowed to marry, or was she not? Was she appointed for life, or was she not? Was she ordained, or was she not? The Lambeth Conferences of 1920 and 1930, prompted by the 1919 report, went a considerable way towards solving these questions (in Resolutions 47-52 and 67-70 respectively). They resolved that the deaconess was allowed to marry, that she was appointed for life, and that she was ordained (though, like the deacon, only in an auxiliary capacity). The Conferences recognised her as a female deacon, but in order to avoid the implication that she could proceed to the priesthood, they ruled that her office 'should follow the lines of the primitive rather than of the modern Diaconate of men'. The Conferences went on to outline her duties, on the pattern of early Church practice, including the right 'with the license of the Bishop, to instruct and preach'. The permission to marry was at variance with the practice of the fourth century, of course, though not with that of the first.[16] The anomaly which remained was the assertion that her diaconate was not the modern diaconate. This made it possible for Anglicans to go on contending (as in revised Canon D 1 of the Church of England) that 'The Order of Deaconesses is not one of the Holy Orders of the Church of England and accordingly Deaconesses may accept membership of any Lay Assembly of the Church of England without prejudice to the standing of their Order'.[17] Resolution 32 of the 1968 Lambeth Conference has now opened the way to the removal of this remaining anomaly, by recommending the revival of the perpetual diaconate, and the recognition of deaconesses as not only true deacons but modern deacons within that context. This would make it possible for most of the discrepancies of function between the deacon and the deaconess to be removed, and for deaconesses to sit in the deliberative assemblies of the clergy, not of the laity,[18] without any implication that they are probationer-priests.

The Limits of Women's Ministry

IN the New Testament, as was universally recognised until modern times, St. Paul sets definite limits to the ministry of women. In 1 Cor. 14: 33-36 he rules that they are not to speak in the congregation: *a fortiori*, therefore, they are not to teach there. The consequence is drawn out explicitly in 1 Tim. 2: 8-15, where he directs that, unlike men, women are not to teach or to lead in prayer. (The supposed inconsistency of this second passage with 1 Cor. 11: 5 is imaginary; if it was when leading in prayer that the Corinthian women removed their veils, St. Paul would naturally say so, but his subject was the removal of veils, and the fact that he does not stop to condemn them also for leading in prayer need not be taken to imply that he approved of this practice.) In both passages he grounds his prohibition on the subordination of women, as taught in the Old Testament, and in the second passage he makes specific appeal to the order of creation and to Gen. 3: 16. The subordination of women is therefore by nature (cf. also 1 Cor. 11: 8-9): it goes back behind the Fall, and still obtains after the coming of Christ. The deductions which St. Paul draws from this subordination are less important than the principle of subordination itself: the deduction that women must not even open their mouths, and the deduction that they must not uncover their heads, both seem to be conditioned by contemporary custom (1 Cor. 11: 16; 14: 33, 36), and the deduction that they must not teach may be similarly conditioned. If so, it would be permissible in changed circumstances for women sometimes to teach, and sometimes to lead in prayer, but not to assume an office in which they would normally do so, and in which they would exercise discipline, since this would be to usurp authority over the menfolk in the congregation. Thus, they should not assume the office of presbyter-bishop, an office which carries with it authority over the congregation (as the title 'overseer' or 'bishop' implies, and as is stated in 1 Thess. 5: 12; 1 Tim. 5: 17; Heb. 13: 17, 24; 1 Pet. 5: 2). Nor should they have a predominant voice in church-government.

The early Church maintained Paul's rule that women should not speak or teach (Tertullian, *Baptism* 17, *Prescription* 41, *Veiling of Virgins* 9; *Didascalia* 15; *Apostolic Constitutions* 3: 6; *Testamentum Domini* 1: 40; Cyril of Jerusalem, *Procatechesis* 14), and further forbade them to administer the sacraments (Tertullian, *loc. cit.*; *Didascalia*, 15, 16; *Apostolic Constitutions* 3: 9). It ordained them to the diaconate but not to the priesthood, and this is not to be attributed to male prejudice, since the early Church freely admitted (as we have seen) that the female deacon could do things for women which the male deacon could not. The examples which later occur in the East of deaconesses exercising a teaching ministry probably reflect a change of custom in the ways of publicly expressing female subordination, and also a growing emphasis on the ministry of the sacraments rather than the ministry of the word as the prime prerogative of the priesthood. To the same two causes may be attributed the striking prominence of lay theologians (women among them) in the Eastern Orthodox Church of today.

Prophetesses were always exempt from the ordinary restriction on teaching, and supposed prophetesses appeared both in the heretical sects of antiquity and in mediaeval Europe. Female preaching was known among the Anabaptists and the early Independents and Methodists, and became common among the Quakers, as it has since become in the Salvation Army and in revivalist movements generally. The Salvation Army was one of the earliest denominations to admit women to its authorised ministry without distinction, though it should be borne in mind that Salvation Army officers do not administer sacraments. The modern emancipation of women has, however, led to a widespread movement towards their ordination, on the same terms as the ordination of men. The universities and the learned professions have been opened to women, and it has been plausibly asked why, if they can study and teach theology at university level, they cannot be ordained.

The Roman Catholic, Orthodox, Old Catholic and Anglican Churches have withstood this movement towards ordination (though the Anglican diocese of Hong Kong has twice taken the opposite line and ordained one or two women, last time with the encouragement of a majority of two in the Anglican Consultative Council), but many Churches of the Congregational and Presbyterian families have now taken the step of ordaining women to the presbyterate. In 1970, some 70 of the 239 member-churches of the World Council of Churches reported that they favoured the ordination of women (24 gave no reply). The Congregational Union of England and Wales took the step of admitting them as long ago as 1917; the Baptist Union of Great Britain and Ireland also took the step some considerable while ago; the Presbyterian Church of England did so more recently; the Church of Scotland did so in 1968, the first ordination taking place in 1969; while the Methodist Conference (GB) resolved in 1966 that the step would be right but that unilateral action would be inexpedient pending the outcome of the Anglican-Methodist union scheme. The Dutch Reformed Church is another church which has recently admitted women to full ordination: it has done so as from the beginning of 1968. Some united Churches ordain women, but not the Church of South India, while the Church of North India, formed in 1970, has declined even to recognise existing women ministers ordained before the union. The three national Lutheran Churches of Scandinavia have now admitted women to the priesthood, but in Norway and particularly in Sweden they have done this under pressure from the state, and opposition continues unabated. In Churches which ordain women, such ordinations are generally few, and in Sweden, where the number is greater, it is balanced by the number of men who have withdrawn in protest.[19]

The authority that women have in the Church is not, of course, determined simply by their opportunities of ordination. The power that they exercised from about the seventh century, particularly through the religious orders, has been exaggerated but was certainly considerable.[20] In our own day, women are increasingly being admitted to a share in Church government,[21] and though it is becoming customary to remove all restrictions here, female representatives give as yet no sign of gaining an undue predominance over male ones.[22]

NOTES

[1] eg Gordon Rattray Taylor, *Sex and Society*.
[2] eg Charles Seltman, *Woman in Antiquity*; J. Cercopino, *Daily Life in Ancient Rome*, ch. iv.
[3] In the report *Women and Holy Orders* (London, CIO, 1966), p. 104.
[4] On the history of this order, and of women's ministry in general, see the elaborate Anglican report of 1919, *The Ministry of Women* (London, SPCK), and J. Daniélou, *The Ministry of Women in the Early Church* (London, Faith Press, 1961).

[5] See Kathleen Bliss, *The Service and Status of Women in the Churches*, p. 110.
[6] See Cyprian, *Dress of Virgins* 7-11; Ambrose, *Virgins* 12.
[7] On asceticism in the first three centuries, see J. O. Hannay, *The Spirit and Origin of Christian Monasticism* (London, Methuen, 1903), chs. 1-3, which must, however, be treated with caution.
[8] On the early history of convent life, see I. Gregory Smith, *Christian Monasticism from the Fourth to the Ninth Centuries* (London, Innes, 1892), pt. 2, ch. 9.
[9] See H. B. Workman, *The Evolution of the Monastic Ideal* (London, Kelly, 1913), pp. 66-74, 302-305. Community of goods has NT precedent, of course (Acts 2:44f; 4:32-5:2), but the NT does not directly connect it with the vocation to poverty.
[10] These sentences are quoted from an unpublished essay by Mother Jane Margaret, CSMV.
[11] On the deaconess of patristic times see, in addition to the literature cited earlier, A. Kalsbach, *Die Altkirchliche Einrichtung der Diakonissen bis zu ihrem Erlöschen* (Freiburg im Breisgau, Herder, 1926).
[12] See Kathleen Bliss, *The Service and Status of Women in the Churches*, pp. 14-15.
[13] For the ancient rites used in ordaining deaconesses, see the 1919 report on *The Ministry of Women*, appendix 14.
[14] On the modern deaconess, see *World Council of Churches Studies No. 4: The Deaconess* (Geneva, WCC, 1966); Kathleen Bliss, *The Service and Status of Women in the Churches*, pp. 79-94, 156-159.
[15] See Kathleen Bliss, *The Service and Status of Women in the Churches*, pp. 36-38, 94-110, 124-131; Kathleen Heasman, *Evangelicals in Action* (London, Bles, 1962).
[16] The canon of the Protestant Episcopal Church in the USA at that time confined the office to virgins and widows, and ruled that it was vacated by marriage. This followed fourth century practice, as modified in the Lutheran Church. The canon was not brought into line with the Lambeth resolutions until 1965.
[17] A similar anomaly exists in the Methodist Church of Great Britain, with the added complication that the Methodist Church does not ordain deacons. The Methodist deaconess, like the Baptist deaconess, is sometimes given the oversight of a congregation, with authority to administer both word and sacraments.
[18] As the report *Women in Ministry* (London, CIO, 1968), p. 47, explicitly proposes.
[19] See the report *Women and Holy Orders*, ch. 4 and Appendix 3B; Kathleen Bliss, *The Service and Status of Women in the Churches*, ch. 4; Fritz Zerbst, *The Office of Women in the Church* (St. Louis, Concordia, 1955), pp. 83-88, 94-95, 100; G. F. Nuttall, *The Holy Spirit in Puritan Faith and Experience* (Oxford, Blackwell, 1946), pp. 87-89. As regards the situation in Sweden, reference may also be made to a remark of Gustav Wingren's, that Bertil Gärtner 'is among the most prolific exegetes in Sweden. He has a considerable influence on young ministers, and in his monographs and essays has rejected on biblical grounds the recent decision of the Church of Sweden to ordain women to the ministry. Alone among Swedish New Testament exegetes (Gösta) Lindeskog takes the opposite and therefore positive standpoint in this question' (*The Main Lines of Development in Systematic Theology and Biblical Interpretation in Scandinavia*, Richmond, Union Theological Seminary in Virginia, 1964, pp. 5-6). See also *The Time is Now* (London, SPCK, 1971), p.39, resolution 28b; Brigalia Bam, ed., *What is Ordination Coming To?* (Geneva, WCC, 1971), pp. 76, 80; *Plan of Church Union in N. India and Pakistan* (4th ed., Madras, CLS, 1965), pp. 13, 56f.
[20] This question may be studied in the 1919 report on the *Ministry of Women*, Appendices 8 and 9.
[21] See Kathleen Bliss, *The Service and Status of Women in the Churches*, ch. 5.
[22] The information which the author of this essay has derived from the authorities quoted above has been supplemented with information supplied by Deaconess Lorna Fry, of the Council for Women's Ministry in the Church; by Miss F. G. Weeks and Miss J. G. Baldwin, of Dalton House, Bristol; by Mrs. V. A. Zander, of the Russian Orthodox Church; and by the Rev. Aksel Solbu, of the Church of Norway. All this the author gratefully acknowledges.

Heresy, Equality and the Rights of Women

MICHAEL BRUCE

The heretical aspect of feminism

THOSE who regard the ordination of women as in practice contrary to the will of God for his Church, though not strictly theologically impossible, could profitably re-read each, or any, essay they may have available which argues positively for the ordination of women, concentrating their attention on the incidental theological opinions expressed, and then judge for themselves whether there is not a pervasive pattern of distortion over a wide field of theology commonly associated with these arguments.

One example must suffice to illustrate the point here: 'The arguments against the ordination of women are indeed based upon Scripture and tradition. But Scripture requires interpretation and tradition is the reflection in the social pattern of those interpreters' views which have gained acceptance at a given moment in history. Until this century, scriptural interpretation and the formation of the consequent tradition has for the most part been in masculine hands, and those almost exclusively, of ordained clergy. It is therefore hardly surprising that (since it was also men who set down the word of the Lord as it came to them) the interpretation and the tradition should have been in favour of male government in society generally and religion in particular.'[1] But why, if this line of argument is to be pursued, stop here? Since our Lord was a man, should he not be suspect also? If, in the interests of feminism, his promise that the Holy Spirit would guide the Church into all truth is to be rejected, not only in relation to tradition, but in relation also to Scripture itself, is not the real demand not just for the ordination of women, but for a new religion?

The assumption in the quotation is that there is a special knowledge independent of the tradition of the Church, and independent even of the Evangelists, by which Scripture and tradition can be judged. This is something quite different from the examining of local and partial traditions in the light of others, in order to grow into the fulness of the living tradition of the Church under the continual guidance of the Holy Spirit. There is a parallel between such special 'knowledge', which enables its possessors to set themselves up in judgment on Holy Scripture itself, and the 'gnosis' of the Gnostic heresies.

Though to describe the rejection of the Divinity of Christ as Arianism, or to describe the denial of His humanity as Docetism, is historically far too great a simplification, as each was more complicated, yet it is true that many, probably most, heresies are like these two—basically concerned with the denial of a single Christian truth.

Many, even of those who are strongly opposed to 'priestesses', have fallen into the error of thinking that there is no heresy involved in the form of feminism which seeks ordination to the priesthood for women, and no theological objection to this extreme demonstration of it, because they have been unable to find any essential Christian belief, which this kind of feminism denies. It is important to remember, however, that not all heresies are of the single-error type, like Docetism and Arianism. It is not easy, for example, to delimit with precision what is the one essential Christian truth which is denied by Gnosticism: yet Gnosticism is a heresy which distorts the Christian Faith.

Feminism,[2] if it is a heresy, must be regarded as a heresy of the second type. To search for a single point of Christian doctrine which feminism denies, in the same way that Arianism denies the divinity of our Lord, is to search for a 'will o' the wisp'; and, indeed, were some such single point to be concentrated upon, neither the danger of feminism, nor the positive truth which it distorts, would be given due importance.

There are those, possibly especially in the Anglican Communion, who regard feminism as a social and political movement, concerned with the franchise and similar questions, but would deny that it is a heresy. They regard 'the priesthood of women as irrelevant . . . very few really believe in it or want it.'[3]

This does not do justice even to the seriousness with which the question of women and the priesthood has been raised within the Anglican Communion;[4] still less does it take account of the extent to which the ministry has been opened to women in the Protestant denominations. Both Roman[5] and Anglican theologians have accepted the validity of the Orders of the Church of Sweden, and, since the action of the Archbishop of Uppsala and others in 'ordaining priestesses' on Palm Sunday 1960, the question can no longer be regarded as academic or irrelevant.

For Roman Catholics, whether they accept the above-mentioned judgment on Swedish Orders or not, the question is whether, if a bishop in the Apostolic Succession, using a valid rite, ordains a woman, she is in fact ordained or not? Is a woman capable of receiving the priesthood?

For Anglicans the question is still more acute, for the Lambeth Conference of 1920, and several Anglican Committees,[6] have accepted the validity of Swedish orders. It is indeed possible for Anglicans to say that these pronouncements were made before the question of priestesses was actual, and cannot therefore be held to express any judgment on the validity of the orders of 'priestesses'; and that, similarly, the Convocation regulations governing permission for 'Swedish ecclesiastics' to preach in Anglican pulpits cannot be held to apply to priestesses. Administratively, then, it may have been wise of the Church of England that it has avoided being rushed into a hasty judgment.[7]

When all has been said as to the propriety of the action of the Swedish Bishops concerned, the theological question as to whether what they did was objectively effective remains. Anglicans indeed have a further obligation to tackle this question, for it was first raised when the Bishop of Hong Kong 'ordained' a woman during the war of 1937-45. The province of the Anglican Communion concerned, the Chung Hua Sheng Kung Hui, did not approve this action, and the woman concerned 'retired';[8] but the theological issue was not faced. It is not enough to brush it aside as irrelevant.

[If this was true when the author wrote, it is doubly true today, for history has now repeated itself. On Advent Sunday 1971, the successor to the Bishop of Hong Kong who laid hands on a deaconess in 1944, and claimed to have ordained her priest, laid hands on two deaconesses, and claimed the same thing. Had the theological issue been faced on the first occasion, there might not have been a second occasion—Ed.]

If there is no theological objection to priestesses, and objection to them is only on the ground of expediency, then it is difficult, if not impossible, to maintain that the objection must hold always and everywhere. If, on the other hand, there is a theological objection, then the contrary belief is a heresy.

What we are concerned with in this book is that form of feminism which in its ultimate manifestation lays claim to the priesthood. Some few Christian doctrines will be examined in relation to the manner in which this sort of feminism involves their distortion. Basically, however, we are concerned with the truth which feminism seeks to assert and, in fact, distorts: the dignity of woman. Historically, feminism arose as a reaction against masculinism:[9] the false idea that the only full members of the human race are male, and that women are second-class members of the human family. Feminism tends to combat this with the claim that women can do all that men can do; that every calling open to men ought to be open to women also. This claim to equality of function has, as its apex, the claim to the priesthood. In this reaction the true dignity of woman, as woman, is obscured, by lowering her to the status of a mere substitute man. The answer to feminism is not a return to the errors of the masculinism which provoked it, but an advance to a new 'women's movement', a real '*women*'s movement', which will restore the true dignity of woman and the balance of mankind.

A practical word of warning is perhaps called for in writing on this subject. This century has already seen a violent reaction against feminism, much uglier than anything that feminism itself has so far produced. It is often forgotten today how much of the early drive of Nazism was anti-feminist, and how enthusiastically this aspect of Nazism was espoused by German girls, as well as boys, in the early days of the movement. It is one of the horrors of feminism that it fails to satisfy either sex, and that therefore unless it is corrected by a true grasp of the dignity of woman in her own right, it will almost inevitably be replaced before long by a reversion to masculinism, which, in the case of Nazism, was more blatant and crude than the original masculinism from which feminism itself was a reaction.

It is not enough to condemn feminism, or even to show where it is wrong. The positive dignity of woman, which feminism misguidedly tries to assert by pretending that men and women are the same, needs to be firmly re-established.

The positive gains—things such as the franchise and educational opportunity, which were suppressed by the Nazis—need to be consolidated, on a sure foundation, on a doctrine of the dignity of woman which has a clear place in the corpus of orthodox Christian teaching.

The positive value of the challenge of feminism is that it is a goad, to stir theologians into dealing more adequately with that aspect of the doctrine of man which is concerned with the fact that mankind was created male and female.

Supporters of the idea of the ordination of women sometimes argue that God might equally well be addressed as 'Mother' as be addressed as 'Father'.[10] They brush aside the argument that this is unbiblical by saying that, in the patriarchal society of biblical days, it was inevitable that God should be thought of as Father, but that, in these enlightened days of real Christian understanding, we know better. But is there any real link between a patriarchal society and the doctrine of the Fatherhood of God; and, if so, why did so many patriarchial societies indulge in the worship of goddesses, and especially of a Great Mother goddess? While, in the Pauline teaching, man as distinct from woman is, in a special sense, made in the image of God.[11]

It is typical of the type of heresy with which we are dealing that this creation of mankind in the image of God should be represented in reverse as God being made in the image of man, *either* male or female, or more subtly in the image of the two sexes held together—a Father-Mother God.

Perhaps even more typical is the fact that those who are infected, or even attracted, by the heresy, are commonly unable to see this distinction. Their basic assumption is that man created God in the image of his fatherhood, and is gradually adding to this conception of God a fuller image of man which includes woman, so that he is slowly learning to think of God as a Father-Mother. The idea that the likeness between God and man springs from an anthropomorphic conception of God is assumed, and there is little awareness that this is diametrically opposed to the biblical view that man is made in the image of God,[12] and that all fatherhood is derived from Him.[13]

It is important to remember that it is not the Father who became incarnate, but the Son. Our knowledge of God is indeed increased as we get to know the Man, Jesus of Nazareth; and the problem for men, of this and every age, is not whether the Man Jesus is big enough to be God, but whether their ideas of God are big enough to fit Jesus. The incarnate Lord did not, however, beget children during his earthly life; he was not the father of an earthly family. He taught his disciples about the Father, he prayed to the Father, he was the express image of the Father;[14] but the 'anthropomorphism' of the incarnation is not an anthropomorphism of Fatherhood.

God the *Son* in his Humanity shows us the nature of God, but it is from the Father that fatherhood is derived. Biological fatherhood does not reveal to us the Fatherhood of God, for this we share with the beasts; but the Fatherhood of God shows us how to grow into that human fatherhood which is distinct from, and higher than, fatherhood in the rest of the animal kingdom.

It is only when we have totally rejected the idea of God made in the image of human fatherhood, or of God as a sort of amalgam of the human sexes, that we can begin to study the mystery of man made in the image of God, without relapsing into heresy.

St. Paul teaches that man, in distinction from woman, is in a special way made in the likeness of God.[15] This point is no incidental aberration, but integral to his teaching about the Godhead[16] and the Church.[17] It does not spring from the woman-hating mind of the Paul of the feminist imagination, but from the Spirit-guided mind of St. Paul the Apostle, whose tender love of women and delicate understanding of them is beyond all measure deeper than feminism. It should be noticed, in passing, that feminists who claim the priesthood for women tend to rely largely on certain texts from St. Paul, while dismissing others as unworthy. On the purely human level, the picture of St. Paul as bogged down in a woman-hating obscurantism, but having rare moments of illumination, when he sees the feminist light, is a distortion which would be funny were it not tragic. St. Paul was a clear thinker. Inconsistency is not a characteristic of his teaching. He was neither deceived by any feminist will o' the wisp, nor was he a misogynist. More seriously, the feminist distortion at this point involves a twisted doctrine of the Holy Spirit, in relation both to Holy Scripture and to the Church. The attempt to abstract a few words of Holy Scripture from their context, and describe these as inspired, while discarding as sub-Christian most of St. Paul's teaching on the relation of the sexes, suggests both that St. Paul was not inspired by the Holy Spirit when he wrote his epistles, and that the Church, the Body of Christ, was not inspired by the Holy Spirit during the long process whereby the *consensus fidelium* sifted out the books to be included in the Canon of Scripture. It further suggests that the teaching that the Church has drawn, all down the ages, and now draws, from these epistles, is not true but false. It is difficult to reconcile any of this with a true doctrine of the Church or of the Holy Spirit.

Perhaps the commonest danger-signal of heretical tendencies is the putting forward of a claim that an opinion held by some Christians against both their fellow Christians on earth, and against the tradition of the Church down the ages, is 'a leading of the Holy Spirit', and that anyone who resists it with reasoned criticism, or caution, is resisting him. Feminists who desire the ordination of women to the priesthood are by no means the only people guilty of this form of spiritual arrogance, which has become all too common among Anglo-Saxons in the past few years. It is, of course, important to remember that any attitude so fundamentally unreasonable as that just described springs, not from the people who adopt it, but from the father of un-reason, who characteristically uses it, not only for the misleading of his dupes, but for the exasperation of others.[18]

Let us return to the Pauline texts mentioned above. In the eleventh chapter of the first Epistle to the Corinthians, St. Paul is dealing with a local and temporary problem.[19] Scholars tell us that it was unheard of, in respectable society, for a woman to appear uncovered in public, and that there was only one class of woman who did so. St. Paul makes what he is referring to abundantly clear, by his reference to the punishment meted out to offenders: 'For, if a woman is not veiled, let her also be shorn; but if it is a shame to a woman to be shorn or shaven, let her be veiled.'

For St. Paul to take vigorous steps to prevent his converts, in the Corinth of the first century, from adopting an attitude towards the current conventions of dress, so lax that it would inevitably have led the outside world to have thought that Christians sat loosely to moral standards, is quite irrelevant to whether women and girls in the twentieth century should be compelled to wear hats in Church.[20] But, if we concede that[21] in this matter of women being covered in Church St. Paul is dealing with a local problem of his own day, can we treat everything that he says, in relation to the question, as part of the local and temporary question? 'But I would have you know, that the head of every man is Christ' . . . 'the head of Christ is God.' Surely these statements are of permanent doctrinal importance; but, sandwiched between them, is 'and the head of the woman is the man'.[22] It is more reasonable and reverent to assume that the Apostle is here enunciating a point of universal truth, which he then applied to the *ad hoc* question, than to think that he allowed his concern for the immediate question so to warp his judgment that he associated a false belief about the relation of the sexes with the very nature of the Godhead.

Those who are infected with the heresy with which we are dealing would, however, contend that it is not just the question of women being uncovered in Church that is the local and temporary question,[23] but that St. Paul is infected through and through with the sub-Christian beliefs of his own time about human relations. What we have to contend with is the pride that rejects obedience and the acknowledgment of headship in all relations. The obedience a wife owes to her husband is rejected, perhaps as frequently by men as by women, because it is obedience itself that is rejected, above all the obedience man owes to God.

St. Paul's other comparison, of the relation between husband and wife, Christ and the Church, brings out a further point: Christ is indeed Master and the Church looks up to him; but what kind of Master? He 'gave himself for it'[24] on the Cross; so must the human husband be willing to give himself for his wife, as she in turn looks up to him.

Thus, the feminism which seeks to iron out the differences between the sexes unwittingly attacks the doctrines both of God and of the Church.

The Christian doctrine of equality

FEW things are less self-evident than the idea that all men are born equal. In mental and physical capacity, heredity distributes its favours with uncompromising distinctiveness. There is a predetermined inequality in the genetic constitution of men.

It is probable, however, that the draughtsmen of the American Constitution were less concerned with biology than with a spiritual concept of equality derived from the Christian religion, even if, for some of them, at second hand. Christians have sometimes argued that it is certain that all men are born equal, since the Bible teaches us, in the Book of Genesis, that God created man in his own image. It would seem, however, that there is no possible basis for the concept of equality on a naturalistic or biological level. Nor is man unique in the realm of nature in this respect. Not only is there an inequality between a cart-horse and a racing thoroughbred, there is also an important inequality between the horse that wins the Derby and the one that does not!

The distinction between 'higher' and 'lower' organisms is one more frequently made and used, in biological science, than it is satisfactorily defined; and it would take us too far from our subject to pursue the question, what it is that makes one organism 'higher' or 'lower' than another. It is sufficient for our purposes to note that there is a broad general agreement between biologists as to the order in which to place organisms, even if they differ widely as to how the terms 'higher' and 'lower' are to be defined. On this broad basis of agreement, it is in general true to say that the 'lower' the organisms, the more equality within the species; the 'higher' the organisms, the more inequality. We will avoid the temptation to pursue the fascinating biological question of the relation of this to the definition of 'higher' and 'lower', and the nature of the evolutionary process. Let it suffice to say that there is more apparent equality between individual red-snow plants than between the rival pumpkins in a country flower show: more equality between individual bacteria in the same infection, than between the gifted and less gifted child in the same human family. In all the realm of nature, men are probably the least equal of all living organisms.

The religious question is not one that we can bring in if we like, to add weight to a concept of equality which is already self-evident on other grounds. The religious question is fundamental.

The Christian doctrine of equality is not the Christianising of a non-religious idea. On the contrary, political and economic ideas of equality are secularisations (not necessarily in a bad sense) of a religious idea. Rousseau, Marx, and many others, are secularisers in the sense that they pursued the idea of equality with a quasi-religious fervour, having lost contact with the roots of the idea in the Hebrew-Christian tradition; while the early leaders of the English Trade Union movement, following a tradition which ran back to the time of the Commonwealth, secularised equality in a different sense, applying, in the secular field of politics and economics, an idea derived from religion.

The historical attribution of the idea of equality to Greece seems, at first sight, more possible; but, here also, there is the formidable difficulty that the equality of the Greek citizen rested on the basis of a slave-owning society. Was there in the Greek idea an inherent force which would ultimately shatter the economic and social basis of any society similar to that in which it was born? Or was the force injected into the idea from Christian conceptions of brotherhood derived from the New Testament?

It is necessary, however, for Christians to remember that if it was Christians, relying on ideas derived from Christianity, who abolished slavery, it was in a society, supposedly Christian for many generations, that they had to struggle to achieve this end. Even amongst Christians, self-evident ideas do not seem to be so self-evident to some people as to others.

We need something more definite, more clear-cut, more like a doctrine, upon which to base our concept of equality, than the secular ideas we have so far considered; for without this, if the old battles have to be re-fought in new circumstances, we may not be adequately armed; and, in the meantime, concepts of equality which are in fact destructive of society, and rooted in nothing but sentimentality, may spread, to the damage both of human relationships and of the true concept of equality itself.

It is interesting to find a book,[25] written from the Christian standpoint, and dealing not least with equality in this secular sense, in relation to sociological, political and economic questions, saying that equality is not a Christian doctrine. I personally think that this statement goes too far, but at least it illustrates the difficulty of the question.

Let me then return to the text in Genesis which seems at first sight to be a hopeful starting-point for the development of such a doctrine. What are we to say about a Christian doctrine of equality based upon the Imago Dei? Are we to base it on only the possible implications of a text which is clearly primarily concerned with another subject, namely, the lordship of man over the animal creation?

Again, the text stating that with our tongue 'bless we God . . . and therewith curse we men, which are made after the similitude of God',[26] is clearly concerned chiefly with the right use of the tongue; but, though reference to the Imago could here too be to men collectively being made in the image of God, it is more natural to read it as implying that each man is made in God's image. If this is to be taken as a part of God's revelation in the New Testament, it is an overwhelming argument in favour of the doctrine of the equality of each individual human soul; for, if all souls are made in the image of God, no other difference between them can obliterate this tremendous fact.

One text, which *can* be interpreted differently, is, however, an insecure foundation upon which to base a doctrine. We must turn to the other evidence which points in the same direction.

Those who have argued in favour of priestesses in the Christian Church, have normally, as Hans Cavallin points out in his essay, laid great stress on Gal.3:28. But, quite apart from the question of priestesses, is this text really concerned with the *equality* of one individual with another at all? It does not say, 'There is neither Jew nor Greek, there is neither bond nor free, there is neither male or female: for ye are all *equal* in Christ Jesus', but 'ye are all *one* in Christ Jesus'. It is again not written in a context in which equality is under consideration. Still less, of course, is the ministry of the Church under consideration.

The irrelevance of the text to the cause which it is dragged out of its context to support could not easily be exaggerated. For the moment, however, we are not concerned with such irrelevancies, but only with the question whether this text gives us the basis for the doctrine of equality for which we are seeking; it must be admitted that it does not. Maybe, given a Christian doctrine of equality, the interpretation of this and similar texts can be deepened and enriched, but it does not of itself form any legitimate basis for such a doctrine.

The caution of Daniel Jenkins and his collaborators in *Equality and Excellence* is clearly not without justification. Indeed, having already stated that there is a Christian doctrine of equality, we have now exhausted the more usual grounds on which it is supposed to rest, without finding any secure foundation for it.

There remain, however, three foundations upon which I believe a Christian doctrine of equality can rest: first, individual responsibility before God, especially moral responsibility; secondly, the individual valuing of sinners by God as worth saving; and thirdly, the equality as members, despite their different functions, of members of the Body of Christ.

There is an indication of the idea of individual responsibility in the regulations for numbering Israel: 'Then shall they give every man a ransom for his soul unto the Lord. . . . This they shall give, every one that passeth among them that are numbered, half a shekel. . . . Every one that passeth among them that are numbered, from twenty years old and above. . . . The rich shall not give more, and the poor shall not give less than half a shekel' (Ex. 30:12-15). This is not the definition of a doctrine of the equality of each human soul in God's sight; but 'the rich shall not give more, and the poor shall not give less' is an indication that each adult Israelite is of equal value in God's sight, and each must pay equally 'a ransom for his soul'.

It is, however, in the moral responsibility, to which we have already referred, that this point comes out more clearly. 'What mean ye, that ye use this proverb concerning the land of Israel, saying, The fathers have eaten sour grapes, and the children's teeth are set on edge?

As I live, saith the Lord God, ye shall not have occasion any more to use this proverb in Israel.

Behold, all souls are mine; as the soul of the father, so also the soul of the son is mine: the soul that sinneth, it shall die' (Ezek. 18:2-4).

'The soul that sinneth, it shall die. The son shall not bear the iniquity of the father, neither shall the father bear the iniquity of the son: the righteousness of the righteous shall be upon him, and the wickedness of the wicked shall be upon him' (Ezek. 18:20).

Here is a clear indication of an individual moral responsibility shared equally by all souls, since all souls are God's.

The same point is driven home in the best loved and most frequently misinterpreted of our Lord's parables. The Good Samaritan was not the man who fell among thieves, but the neighbour who ministered to him. 'What shall I do to inherit eternal life?' The parable is the story of one of the despised Samaritans fulfilling the love of our neighbours which the lawyer has himself described as being part of the requirement for the inheritance of eternal life.

Samaritans, like Jews, have the same moral obligations laid upon them; and surely, in the context, it is implicit that they have also the same religious obligation to love God, and the same potentiality to inherit eternal life. The emphasis, however, is on an equality of moral obligation which, if it includes Samaritans as well as Jews, includes all mankind.

As all men share equally a moral obligation, so we find St. Paul teaching in the Epistle to the Romans that all have failed: 'for all have sinned, and come short of the glory of God' (Rom. 3:22-23). The equality of obligation leads to an equality of need, which in turn leads to the second basis for a Christian doctrine of equality, the valuing of all souls equally by God, in that Christ was willing to die for all equally. St. Paul refers to this in the immediate context of the text just quoted. 'For all alike have sinned, and are deprived of the divine splendour, and all are justified by God's free grace alone, through his act of liberation in the person of Christ Jesus' (Rom. 3:23-24 NEB). The care of God for each individual human soul is so written all over the New Testament that it will suffice to mention the twin parables of the Lost Sheep and the Lost Coin.

Yet, strong as is the emphasis on the value of the individual soul, this second basis of the Christian doctrine of equality is in no way inconsistent with the third: all those who are baptised into Christ are equally members of his Body. Indeed, the twin parables just referred to owe a part of their emphasis on the value of the individual to the setting of the individual within the whole. The ninety and nine are incomplete without the lost sheep to make up the hundred of the complete flock. The lost coin was more likely to be one of a set of ten, in an ornament, than merely one of ten loose coins in a purse. The ornament would be spoiled with one coin missing, and this was almost as unlucky as losing a wedding ring. The tenth coin was needed to make up the set.

So the members of the body, which Paul refers to in the twelfth chapter of the First Epistle to Corinthians,[27] are all equally members of the body, are all equally dependent on each other, and all equally suffer if one suffers.

We have reached, then, a Christian doctrine of equality, firmly based in the theology of Creation and Redemption; but it must be admitted that it has little resemblance to the secular ideas of equality which have dominated the twentieth century mind.

All human souls are equal, for all equally have a moral responsibility. All human souls are equal, for God valued all equally in thinking each worth Christ's dying for. All human souls are equal, for all were created in their freedom, equally capable of reflecting that love which is God's nature, and of becoming members of Christ's Church.

This equality of value is, however, set within an infinite variety of function. The twelfth chapter of the First Epistle to the Corinthians expressly rejects the idea of a body consisting all of eyes or all of ears.[27]

Every human soul is indeed of equal value in the sight of God, whether it be the soul of the Queen or of a kitchen-maid, of the Prime Minister or of a railway porter, whether it be of a man or of a woman; but it is no part of the Christian doctrine of equality that all Queens must be kitchen-maids, all railway porters Prime Ministers, or all women men. On the contrary, not only are there different callings—apostles, prophets, teachers, etc. (1 Cor. 12:28)—but each individual soul, because he is a member of the Body, has his own individual and unique place within it.

The corruptions of the Christian doctrine of equality totally distort it, making of it an instrument of division, based on personal, class and group greed. This corruption is the just and natural result and penalty of trying to enjoy the fruits of a Christian culture, when the Christian religion has been forsaken. Most of those in the modern world who struggle and fight for equality have lost sight of the roots of equality in Redemption and Creation, since they have lost sight of the Redeemer and Creator. Inevitably this leads to the twisting of an equality of value into a supposed equality of function. Such an equality has no foundation in fact, reason, or Christian teaching; but true equality is so precious a thing that this strange, unreal perversion of it can evoke the emotion of loyalty. As we have seen already, however, the corruption does not normally rest at the stage of emotional support for a chimera. Soon, equality of different interdependent members of one Body is distorted into bitter quarrels for equality of pay, or equality of status, between independent individuals. Mutual hatred and suspicion spring from the ugly, selfish struggle for personal gain or advantage.

The Christian doctrine of equality presupposes a dependence on, and the service of, other people in the spirit of love. There is a spirit of acceptance on the one hand, and generosity on the other, which reflects in terms of human life the perfect equality and unity in love within the Godhead.

The struggle for higher status, which is too often a characteristic of the humanist search for equality, has no parallel in the perfect unity of the Godhead.

Equality and humility

'LET your bearing towards one another arise out of your life in Christ Jesus. For the divine nature was his from the first; yet he did not think to snatch at equality with God, but made himself nothing, assuming the nature of a slave. Bearing the human likeness, revealed in human shape, he humbled himself, and in obedience accepted even death—death on a cross' (Phil. 2:5-9 NEB).

To feel the force of this, we need to set it beside the doctrinal statement of the Church's faith in regard to the equality of the Three Persons in the Blessed Trinity. 'And in this Trinity none is afore, or after other: none is greater, or less than another; But the whole three Persons are co-eternal together: and co-equal' (*Quicunque Vult*).

Our Lord is 'Equal to the Father, as touching his Godhead: and inferior to the Father, as touching his Manhood' (*Quicunque Vult*).

The difficulty of reconciling these quotations is not primarily intellectual but moral; human pride so distorts the idea of equality that it stubbornly resists the notion that equality and humility can go together.

The Father sent the Son into the world,[28] but this sending was not the sending of a slave. He who was equal to the Father 'took on him the form of a servant' (assumed the nature of a slave, in NEB), but of his own free will he emptied himself of his heavenly glory to become man.

The unity of God is unspoilt by any pride or selfishness of the Three Persons towards each other. The Son does not regard it as beneath his dignity to be obedient to the Father, nor the Father seek to assert himself by tyrannising over the Son.

It is by no means only in the claim that women should be admitted to the priesthood that the Christian doctrine of equality is abused. Twentieth century society is riddled with false conceptions of equality, rooted in pride and envy, and bearing fruit in division and bitterness. It is all too probable that the end of this century, or the beginning of the next, will see a violent reaction towards a hierarchical society, in which men will seek escape from the loneliness of modern man. The fact that this century has already seen the rise of a hideously ugly reaction of this sort, which it required a world war to destroy, should make those who espouse the cause of equality careful lest they so misintepret it as to pave the way for a new Nazism: and those who believe in a hierarchical society, careful lest, in opposing false ideas of equality, they oppose equality itself.

It is perhaps not irrelevant that it is those countries which are most self-consciously dedicated to egalitarian theory that have had cause to complain of 'the cult of personality' within them. Let it suffice at this point to say that men on the whole, however much they approve of modesty, do not associate it with a driving ambition towards greatness.

Yet, in Christian belief, it is Jesus, our Lord and Master, the greatest Man who has ever lived, the summit of human dignity, who is the supreme exemplar of humility.

'Ye call me Master and Lord,' says Jesus in the account in the Gospel according to St. John of His washing the disciples' feet (Jn. 13: 2-10) "and so I am".'

The fact that he was so called, and that he accepted and approved being so called, and yet humbled himself to wash the disciples' feet—the work of the humblest slave—seems to the natural man a paradox. Dignity and humility tend to be contrasted. Great men are commended when they treat ordinary folk as fellow human beings. 'So friendly and unassuming' will be the comment of many people on a first meeting with, perhaps, a member of the British royal family, or with one of those members of the aristocracy who seek to live up to the tradition *noblesse oblige;* but the tone of surprise betokens the fact that they do not naturally associate an unassuming manner with greatness.

Again, Jesus avoided attempts to make him king (Jn. 6:15). When Pilate asked if he were a king, though he did not deny it, he made clear that the word was not his choice, and when he went on to speak of his kingdom he explained that it was not one of earthly power and glory. In a similar way his divine glory is not denied, but is hidden rather than published abroad. It is impossible, then, for us as Christians to accept the world's estimate of the nature of dignity. Nor is it possible for us to brush dignity aside as though it had no place in Christian thinking. The dignity of God in Christ was revealed in the humility of Jesus of Nazareth.

But if Christian dignity is revealed in humility, it is not revealed in the seeking of status. The desire for the priesthood as a status-symbol would instantly disqualify any individual male candidate, and the desire for the priesthood for women *as a status-symbol* of equality with men is equally improper.

It is one thing to recognise the all too pervasive infection of pride, and the danger of its corrupting even the noblest of vocations, either by lurking as a 'hidden' ambitious 'mixed motive' or by tempting into a domineering attitude. It is quite another to elevate such temptations to being, not a danger inherent in the priestly vocation, but a part of the vocation itself.[29]

The dangers are real, and against them every Bishop, every priest, deacon and theological student needs constantly to be on guard. For if a vocation may survive and even be strengthened by battling against the subtle temptations to pride inherent in the work of a priest, yet any persistent acceptance by the will of the lust for status, or any other form of pride, will wholly and utterly corrupt any vocation to the priesthood, poison the man's work, and, if not repented of, bring his soul to hell.

When this lust for status occurs in women, not merely as a temptation, but as an accepted aim, it can be no more sinful than it is in man. What is wholly corrupt in essence cannot be made more corrupt by being in one sex rather than in another; but it has an even deeper quality of tragedy, for, as well as its individual sinfulness, it is in a special sense a betrayal of her sex and an abandonment of her calling. It reduces woman to being a mere substitute for man in a pitiful unawareness of her own different and parallel dignity. From the utter humility of the Blessed Virgin's 'Behold the handmaid of the Lord', saint after saint of her sex has followed her in the abandonment of status, and thereby has inspired by her humility not merely her own sex but the whole Body of Christ.

It is of course true that all the saints set before us the example of humility, but it is to the women saints that we turn, not perhaps for the brilliant example of heroic struggles in which pride is abandoned and humility accepted, but for the steady light of continuous unfailing acceptance of humble dependence on God.

It is these women who reveal in its splendour the dignity of woman. It is they who command, without ever asking for it, or wanting it, the reverence of mankind, and not least of men. It is their example which has given, and continues to give, to the priesthood the greatest encouragement: it is their prayers that give the greatest help.

NOTES

[1] Mrs. Baxter in *Women & Holy Orders*, Church Information Office, 1966, p. 119.

[2] It is only the type of feminism which culminates in wanting the priesthood for women that is here implied. 'Feminism' is sometimes

used, as we shall see, to cover resistance to the denial of the basic Christian doctrine of equality. I question whether this is a proper use of the term. It certainly is not the sense in which I use it here.

[3] The quotation is from a letter from a very able woman who occupied an important position in the training of women for the service of the Church in the Anglican Communion.

[4] More recently the issue has also been raised in the Church of Rome.

[5] 'L'Eglise Suedoise d'Etat a-t-elle garde la Succession Apostolique?' by L. -M. Dewailly O. P., in *Revue des Sciences Philosophiques et Theologiques*, July 1938; 'Die apostolische Succession in Schweden', by Theodor van Haag S. J., in *Kyrkohistorisk Arsskrift*, 1944; *The Church of England and the Church of Sweden* (Report of the Archbishop's Commission under the chairmanship of Bishop Ryle), A. R. Mowbray, 1911.

[6] *The Church of England and the Church of Sweden* (Report of the Archbishop's Commission), Mowbray, 1911; Lambeth Conference 1920; *Relations with the Church of Sweden* (Report of the Archbishop of Canterbury's Committee, 1954).

[7] 'The Church of Sweden' (Report of the Lower House of Canterbury Convocation Committee), 1961.

[8] She returned to her work as a deaconess, which she fulfilled with faithfulness and devotion.

[9] Professor V. A. Demant, in his essay 'Why the Christian Priesthood is Male', in *Women & Holy Orders*, argues persuasively that the reaction is really an extension of the disease, a thought which underlines the importance of the dangers referred to in the next paragraph.

[10] Mrs. Baxter in 'The Case for the Ordination of Women to the Priesthood' in *Women & Holy Orders* does not go so far as this, but she writes: ' . . . the material image of God is found in the Old Testament (Isa. 49:15; 66:13) as well as that of the Father.' Reference to these texts, and a comparison with the frequency of 'Father' in the words of Jesus in the New Testament, is instructive.

[11] 1 Cor. 11:7.
[12] Gen. 1:27.
[13] Eph. 3:15.
[14] Heb. 1:3.
[15] 1 Cor. 11:7.
[16] 1 Cor. 11:3.
[17] Eph. 5:22-33.
[18] e.g. V. A. Demant in 'Why the Christian Priesthood is Male' (*Women & Holy Orders*): ' . . . those who contest for the addition of a female ministry to the male one believe that what they take for the spirit of the Age (Zeitgeist) is identical with the Holy Spirit (Heilige Geist) who always gets involved in support of what one likes to believe!' This is mild. Orthodox Christians can get far more

exasperated than this.

[19] 1 Cor. 11:5-6.

[20] St. Paul would probably have been equally as shocked by modern hats as by bare heads.

[21] It may be of interest to put on record the story behind the joint statement of the Archbishop of Canterbury and York issued during the Second World War, permitting women and girls to come to Church bare headed. When the King called for a National Day of Prayer on the anniversary of the beginning of the war, people were urged to pray in any near by Church at some time during the day. The Day of Prayer was a weekday and what was visualised was that people would visit a church on their way to or from work or during their lunch hour. The present writer wrote to Archbishop Temple, pointing out that vast numbers of girls working in the munition and other factories, even if they owned hats, which many did not, certainly would not dream of going to work in one, and would be inhibited from carrying out the suggestion of going to church to pray, by the belief that no woman was allowed to enter a church without a hat. I asked for a statement, not merely removing the supposed ban, but such as would also relieve tender consciences, and show that the practice of girls going bare headed to church (which had for years been the custom in Anglican Churches in China) was not contrary to the Bible. Time proved too short to get a statement out before the Day of Prayer, but the Archbishop's promise that he would deal with the matter was soon fulfilled.

[22] 1 Cor. 11:3.

[23] The question as to what is of merely temporary importance and what is of permanent importance is raised in another manner in relation to our Lord himself. Not only psychologically but also physically our Lord could not have chosen tea, or any of the non-alcholic beverages made possible by modern science, as alternatives to wine for the Holy Eucharist. It would therefore be nonsense to argue that they should not be used for Holy Communion, because our Lord would have provided for their use had he meant this to happen. But is this to say that what he in fact used is not for us binding? May not the scandal of particularity in the choice of Israel, Bethlehem, the first century and the Incarnation itself, run on into the choice of the matter and the minister of the sacraments?

[24] Eph. 5:2.

[25] *Equality and Excellence*, by Daniel Jenkins, SCM, 1961.

[26] Jas. 3:9.

[27] 1 Cor. 12:12ff.

[28] Gal. 4:4; John 3:17; 4:34; 5:23,24,30,36,37,38; 6:29 etc.

[29] See Mrs. Baxter in *Women & Holy Orders*, p. 118.

The Priestess in the Greco-Roman World

Edward R. Hardy

THE WORD *sacerdos* in Latin is epicene, whereas the Greek ἱερεύς is capable of a feminine form, ἱερεια. In either language the Greco-Roman world was acquainted with female as well as male sacred personages, though these would not in every case be priests in the sense of offerers of sacrifices. The most conspicuous were the Vestal Virgins at Rome, who as guardians of the sacred fire probably represented the king's daughters who had tended the hearth in the days when the king of Rome was the chief of a primitive clan by the Tiber. Selected between the age of six and ten for thirty years service, after which they could leave and marry (but often did not), they lived in dignity in the Atrium Vestae of which the remains may still be seen in the Forum. The fire in Vesta's shrine was annually rekindled by a priest on the first of March, the old Roman New Year's Day; during the festival of Vesta in June the sacred store-room was open to the visits of matrons, and at its climax the year's ashes were removed. The Vestals took part in various traditional festivals, most of which seem originally to have an agricultural character, though why on May 15th the Pontifex Maximus and the wife of the Flamen Dialis joined them in a procession of which the climax was throwing straw effigies into the Tiber was as great a mystery to the Romans of the Empire as it is to us. As sacrosanct figures the Vestals were guardians of wills, and were credited even by the sceptical with special powers of intercession—*redimunt vitam populi procrumque salutem* is a Christian poet's description of the pagan belief.[1] Besides a considerable endowment, their privileges included the right to use wheeled vehicles within the City, and special seats at the gladiatorial games, which other women would watch only from the back rows. To us this seems a strange form of entertainment for virgins (as it did to Prudentius in the fourth century), but the reason behind it may be the original sacred character of the games as a sacrifice of captives. The Vestals were not admitted to athletic contests until Nero discovered that this privilege was allowed to their approximate Greek counterpart, the priestess of Demeter at Olympia, who sat on the altar during the Olympic games.[2]

The Atrium Vestae was adorned with statues of honoured members of the community. A typical inscription says of a mid-third century Chief Vestal (*Virgo Vestalis maxima*) that the state felt daily the effects of her chastity (*disciplina*) and exactitude in fulfilling the sacred rites.[3] The virginity of the Vestals seems to have been valued more as a means of preserving their semi-magical potency as daughters of the State than as a form of ascetic devotion. When Domitian revived the half-forgotten penalty of burial alive for the 'incest' of a Vestal,[4] the Roman world was startled but not apparently shocked. The episode is suggestive of Thomas Cromwell's career as an enforcer of monastic discipline, but it may reflect the supersitition rather than the wickedness of the Emperor. Perhaps as much may be said for the execution of Vestals under Caracalla, though one cannot take very seriously the claim of Elagabalus that he was justified in marrying a Vestal since as a priest he could properly marry a priestess.[5] Besides the Roman Vestals there were similar colleges in other Italian towns. It was for a Vestal of Alba and her lover that, probably in the 370's, Symmachus, the pagan leader of the Roman Senate, petitioned for the establishment of a proper tribunal, though he can scarcely have secured this in the days of Christian Emperors.[6] The Roman college seems to have been respectable enough in its later days, in which it enters briefly into comparison with the virgins of the Church. After the disendowment of Roman paganism by Gratian in 382, Symmachus pleaded for the Vestals as well as for the other pagan institutions in his petition for the restoration of the altar of Victory addressed to Valentinian II in 384. Ambrose and Prudentius rather ungenerously replied that the pagans could only support six or seven virgins (the extra one presumably a novice) at great expense while the Church easily produced hundreds.[7] The only obvious point of similarity would seem to be that virgins and widows were expected to maintain the Church by their prayers.[8] Losing apparently some of its members to the Church, the College of Vestals survived disendowment until the final suppression of public paganism at Rome by Theodosius in 394.[9]

Greece and Egypt

ROME itself does not seem to have had any other fulltime priestesses, although women did offer sacrifice at the strictly female mysteries of the Good Goddess, celebrated in the house of one of the magistrates in December. The wife of the priest of Jupiter, *flamen dialis*, was *flaminica dialis*, and like her husband subject to various obscure taboos. She appeared at some of the festivals celebrated by the Vestals, but was not considered a priestess of Juno as some have supposed. In Greece matters were somewhat different, since it seemed natural to the Greek mind that a goddess should be served by a priestess. There was some hesitation on the matter, however. A collection of evidence on the subject assembles references to 171 priestesses and 177 priests of various goddesses (while priestesses of gods were very rare, though not entirely unknown).[10] The status of the Greek priestess, like that of the Greek priest, varied. She might be an attendant at the temple, she might be a member of a distinguished family taking part in a civic festival, she might be a child or young woman in a semi-dramatic role. A few examples may serve to illustrate. At Eleusis the priestess of Demeter formally presided at the shrine, although the hierophant who conducted the initiation into the mysteries was more conspicuous. At Delphi the roles were reversed, since the priest of Apollo was the chief figure, but the Pythia (of whom more later) was the voice of the oracle. At Corinth Poseidon was served by a maiden priestess until she was ready for marriage; while in the country at Orchomenus the shrine of Artemis had been attended by a virgin until sad experience indicated that a widow would be safer.[11] At Sparta the young maidens who served the shrine of the Leucippides, daughters of Apollo, were also called Leucippides; at Patrae the virgin selected annually as priestess of Artemis rode behind deer in the procession, and there was a similar impersonation at Tegea.[12] And a rash soul who attempted violent entry into the Acropolis at Athens might be met by the priestess of Athena Polias on her throne, apparently as living representative of the goddess.[13]

Besides the traditional cult priestesses one must note the honorific priesthoods of ruler-cults; the deified females of the Ptolemaic house received honorary priestesses at Alexandria and Ptolemais,[14] and the custom was carried to the Roman world with the deification of Augustus' wife Livia, followed by several imperial ladies of the second century.[15] These offices seem to have been civic distinctions, secured by leading citizens for their debutante daughters, and involved no more serious sacerdotal functions than those of the young ladies carrying baskets who appear in the Parthenon sculptures. The importance of the mysteries devoted to a female deity, the Great Mother and Isis, might have led one to expect a similar importance of women in their cult, but this does not seem to have followed. In Egypt women are found in the lower ranks of the priesthood, the Levites of the Egyptian temples as it were, as singers and dancers—a conspicuous case is that of the twins Thaues and Taus, attached to the Serapeum at Memphis with the duties of pouring libations for the dead and wailing for Apis, who figured in legal proceedings in the second century BC.[16] But the bride of Amon whom Herodotus had heard of at Thebes belonged to the past, and it was centuries before that the later Pharaohs had replaced the highpriest of Amon by a succession of princesses as Divine Votaresses, which seems to have been a means of keeping under their control a dangerous centre of power which in previous ages had threatened the throne.[17] After all, the cult of Isis was ultimately derived from that of Osiris, and if women were prominent among her worshippers, descriptions, pictures, and documents show her as mainly served by men. There are a few exceptions, such as the female 'interpreter of dreams' who appears at Athens; and several monuments show women in the costume of the goddess carrying her sistrum and rattle.[18] These are probably to be interpreted as patronesses of the cult who were given an honorific position. If they have a parallel in the Church it is to be found in the honourable women for whom a place of distinction was found in the congregation, and who are sometimes called διακονοι or πρεσβυτιδες—from the Phoebe of Romans 16, whom I would put in this category, to the wealthy deaconess Olympias who was one of St. Chrysostom's friends and supporters at Constantinople.[19]

In areas under oriental influence more startling phenomena appear, when the awe inspired by the life-force takes surprising and sometimes disgusting forms. Sacred prostitution existed in Western Asia in ancient times, as in modern India, and was naturally as repulsive to Christians as to Jews in the period with which we are concerned. I suspect, however, that ancient and modern writers have sometimes seen the institution on slight evidence; it is certainly frequently referred to as something practised far away or long ago.[20] Herodotus may have been well-informed when he tells us that at Babylon and in Cyprus women thought it proper to lose their virginity in a temple, and Strabo when he reports the same practice at a shrine of Anaitis in Armenia,[21] but one wonders a bit. However, Lucian reports from his own time that women at Byblos who refused to mourn for Adonis were obliged to give themselves to strangers;[22] and similar customs seem to have survived at Heliopolis (Baalbek) until suppressed by Constantine, although Athanasius refers to sacred prostitution in Phoenicia as a thing of the past.[23] Back in the first century, Strabo doubtless knew the habits of the sacred women of the god Ma at Comana in Pontus near his homeland, to whom he compares the hetaerae of Corinth, sacred to Aphrodite.[24] But he is here referring to old Corinth, destroyed by the Romans in 146 BC, and not to the new Roman colony of his own time. It does not seem that the Corinth of St. Paul and the Rome of St. Peter needed any such cover for their licentiousness; when Juvenal observes in passing 'in front of what temple won't you find a woman?' (*nam quo non prostat femina templo*)[25] he is, I think, referring to the temples of Rome as places of public resort.

Response to inspiration

CLOSER to possible Christian experience are the women who re-

sponded to some form of divine inspiration. In the procession
described by Apuleius the female devotees of Isis at Corinth seem to
be dignified ladies with perfumed hair and veils. But with references
to the Bacchae of the same city Pausanias cautiously observes 'they
say the women are sacred and maddened by Dionysus'.[26] As a modern
writer puts it, the Bacchae were not priestesses but 'worshippers who
stood in a very close relation to the god'. We are not far away in
time, place, or phenomenon from the more disorderly aspects of the
life of the early Corinthian church. And not far away was the Pythia
of Delphi who, in the words of the learned lady just quoted, 'owed her
position to the excitable temperament of womanhood' as well as to
the water of the sacred spring.[27] Lucian satirically invites us to
sympathise with the hard-worked Apollo who had to rush from
oracle to oracle 'at the beck of every priestess who has taken her
draught of holy water, munched the laurel-leaf, and made the tripod
rock', and casually refers to the maddened women to be found with
the throng of priests and assistants at the great temple of Hierapolis.[28]
More respectfully, Strabo speaks of the θεοφερητοι, those carried
away by divinity, at the Cappadocian shrines—we are not very far here
from Ignatius of Antioch who was also θεοφορος—and mentions
that at Castabala the priestesses of 'Perasian Artemis' walked barefoot
over coals,[29] a performance to which there are of course modern
parallels in various parts of the world. From this Anatolian world
have arisen both Christian and Moslem representatives of the 'enthusiasm' which the eighteenth century so much deplored, and in which
women have had their part. One thinks of the prophetesses who were
supporters, almost colleagues, of the Phrygian heresiarch Montanus,
and of the nameless third century woman, the Joanna Southcott or
Aimee Semple Macpherson of her time, who claimed by prophetic
authority to organise her own sect in which she professed to administer
the rites of the Church, including both Baptism and the Eucharist.
We know of her because in writing to Cyprian Bishop Firmilian of
Caesarea quoted this as an instance of heretical baptism which could
not possibly be valid.[30] Probably from the same area came the
Marcosian Gnostic who according to Irenaeus imposed on the silly
women of Gaul by the impressive ceremonies in which he invited
some of them to bless lesser cups, and then himself made the eucharistic
cup turn pink, presumably by the addition of some chemical.[31]

Early Christians

IF we ask why the early Church did not invite women to preside at
the Eucharist, the most definitely priestly act of the Christian ministry,
the answer undoubtedly is that for a number of reasons the idea never
occurred to it. Ceremonially the ἐπισκοπος at the Eucharist succeeds

to the Jewish *paterfamilias* saying grace; and spiritually to the Jewish priest presenting offerings to the Lord in a religion which did not know priestesses, though it did recognise that prophetic inspiration could come to either sex. Such formal discussion as we find in ancient Christian writers seems to revolve around the question whether a woman might conceivably administer Baptism, probably because they were used to solemn baptisms celebrated by the Bishop and his attending presbyters, with deacons and (in some places at least) deaconesses assisting in the actual undressing and immersion of the candidates. Tertullian suggests that if heresy were unrestrained, it might lead to women's venturing to exorcise and baptise;[32] Firmilian tells us that this actually occurred, as noted, and Epiphanius of Salamis includes in his magnificent catalogue of heresies a branch of the Montanists who had female presbyters and bishops.[33] In the mid-third century the author of the *Didascalia Apostolorum* argues that the duty of widows was to pray, not to teach or baptise; and a century later the editor of the *Apostolic Constitutions* enlarges this passage with the note that while women might visit the sick and lay hands on them, the Church did not have priestesses, unlike the Gentiles with their female deities.[34] Finally, in the late fourth century Epiphanius takes up the ministry of women when at the end of his collection of heresies he comes to the Collyridians, a sect of Thracian origin whose women had the curious custom of offering cakes to the Virgin Mary. Besides pointing out that Mary is venerated but not worshipped, he observes that neither under the old covenant or the new was the priestly office given to women, although the possibility of a female prophet was guaranteed by the case of the four daughters of Philip the Evangelist (Acts 21: 9). Surely no one in the Church was more deserving of honour than Mary, yet it was the Apostles who first celebrated the Eucharist and John the Baptist who baptised her Son. In his own time the Church used the ministry of deaconesses, primarily he thinks for attendance on female candidates at Baptism, but if it did call some women πρεσβυτιδες this is an honorary rank and does not make them female presbyters or priestesses.[35] And what Epiphanius stated remained the general attitude of the Church.

Notes

[1] Prudentius, *Contra Symmachum* ii. 1104; on the Vestals see J. P. V. Balsdon, *Roman Women*, 1962, pp. 235-242; W. Warde Fowler, *The Roman Festivals of the Period of the Republic*, 1899, *s.v.*; Thomas Cato Worsfold, *The History of the Vestal Virgins of Rome*, a scrappy but useful collection of information.

[2] Suetonius, *Augustus* 44. 3; *Nero* 12. 4; Pausanias, *Description of Greece*, vi. 20,9.

[3] Dessau, *Inscriptiones Latinae Selectae* 4932.
[4] Suetonius, *Domitian* 8,4; Pliny the Younger, *Epistolae* iv.11.
[5] Herodian, *Ab Excessu Divi Marci* iv. 6,4; v. 6,2.
[6] Symmachus, *Epistolae* ix. 147-8.
[7] Ambrose, *Epistolae* 18. 11-12, replying to Symmachus, *Relatio ad Valentinianum;* Prudentius, *Contra Symmachum* ii. 910-1,132.
[8] cf., Hippolytus, *Apostolic Tradition* 11; *Didascalia Apostolorum* 14 and 15.
[9] The pagan Zosimus (v. 38) ends their history with a story of the last Vestal's curse, against the wife of Stilicho.
[10] Elizabeth Sinclair Holderman, *A Study of the Greek Priestess*, Michigan, 1913, p. 8.
[11] Pausanias ii. 33,2; vii. 5,11.
[12] Pausanias vii. 18,12; viii. 53,3.
[13] Herodotus, *History* v. 72.
[14] W. Otto, *Priester und Tempel im hellenistischen Aegypten*, vol. i, 1905, pp. 157-8, 162-3; list of known incumbents pp. 185-193, 195-6.
[15] Balsdon, *op. cit.* pp. 243, 249-251.
[16] Otto, *op. cit.* pp. 92-3, 102-3; cf., Edwyn Bevan, *A History of Egypt under the Ptolemaic Dynasty*, 1927, pp. 297-8.
[17] Herodotus i. 182; cf., Hermann Kees, *Das Priestertum im Aegyptischen Staat vom neuen Reich bis zur Spätzeit*, 1953, pp. 203-5.
[18] cf., Georges Lafarge, *Histoire du Culte des Divinités d'Alexandrie*, 1884, pp. 139-40, monuments 85-89, 113-115.
[19] Sozomen, *Historia Ecclesiastica*, viii. 9.
[20] J. G. Frazer, *Adonis Attis Osiris*, 3rd ed. 1914, chapters 3-4, assembles and I think somewhat exaggerates the evidence.
[21] Herodotus i. 199; Strabo, *Geography* xi. 14,16.
[22] *De Dea Syria* 6.
[23] Eusebius, *Vita Constantini* iii. 58; Athanasius, *Contra Gentes* 26.
[24] Strabo xii. 3,36.
[25] *Satires* ix. 24.
[26] Apuleius, *Golden Ass* xi. 10; Pausanias ii. 7,5.
[27] Holderman, *op. cit.* p. 19.
[28] *Bis Accusatus* 1; *De Dea Syria* 43.
[29] xii. 2,3 and 7; 3,32.
[30] Firmilian's letter in Cyprian, *Epistolae* 74 (75) 10-11.
[31] *Adversus Haereses* i. 13.
[32] *De Praescriptione* 41.
[33] *Panarion*, Heresy 49.2.
[34] *Didascalia* 15, expanded in *Apostolic Constititions* iii. 9.
[35] *Panarion*, Heresy 79. 2-4; doubtless to avoid such confusions the Council of Laodicea (c. 350?) had ordered that no more πρεσβυτιδες be appointed (Canon 11).

The Office of Woman in the New Testament

GEORG GUNTER BLUM

1 Indications of services rendered by women in the life of Jesus

THERE ARE NO direct statements by either the earthly or the Risen Christ on the position of women in the Christian community. In spite of this, the question as to the attitude of Jesus to women is both justified and significant. Although there is no answer either in developed teaching or in single statements, yet certain conclusions can be drawn from particular situations in the life of Jesus.

The influence of Jesus, by word and deed, was exercised on both men and women without distinction. The Gospels depict for us a series of encounters of our Lord with women, and we are shown emphatically that it was precisely the women who were honoured by his miracles and his revealing teaching.[1] But of greater importance is the fact that a small group of women lived constantly in the society of Jesus and followed him, just as did the disciples. Luke the Evangelist emphasises this fact, and refers to it in one of his summarised reports of Jesus's activity: 'And the twelve were with him, and certain women, which had been healed of evil spirits and infirmities, Mary called Magdalene, out of whom went seven devils, and Joanna, the wife of Chuza Herod's steward, and Susanna, and many others which ministered unto him of their substance' (Luke 8:1-3). This report is not exclusive to Luke, nor is it according to a specially Lukan construction. Mark also speaks of several women who were witnesses of the Crucifixion, 'Who also, when he was in Galilee, followed him and ministered unto him' (Mark 15:40ff).[2] In the same way as Luke, he mentions a particular service which these women rendered in the company of Jesus. They regarded it as their duty to minister to Jesus and to his disciples of their substance (τὰ ὑπάρχοντα). What is significant is that various women are mentioned by name, an indication of their high reputation and the historical authenticity of their mention.[3] Thus it is unlikely that this is a case of reading back into the life of Jesus a primitive Christian occurrence, but rather a note which completely corresponds to historical facts. It is hardly possible to regard this ministering by women as a preliminary stage of the early Christian office of deaconess. It would be better to speak of typological reference to this office. It is conspicuous that Luke, otherwise so pro-feminine, expressly avoids the feminine form of the term 'disciple', probably of set purpose, as he wishes to restrict the number of disciples to the inner circle of the Twelve and the wider circle of the Seventy.[4] The women who ministered to Jesus and his disciples of their substance were not called and commissioned specially, as were the disciples. The reason for their ministry lies entirely in their experience of healing from the power of evil spirits and of infirmities.[5]

As during his earthly life, women play a significant part after his Resurrection. In the synoptic Gospels and in John the women near Jesus are not only concerned with his burial,[6] but are also the first to discover the empty tomb;[7] it is they who encounter the Risen Lord and his angels[8] respectively, and who bring the news of the Resurrection to the disciples.[9] Although this fulfils a fundamental condition of the apostolate, namely the meeting with the Risen Lord, and although Mary Magdalene is vouchsafed a special appearance,[10] there were no women-Apostles, just as there were no women-disciples. Important as was the part played by women in the earthly life of Jesus, and as witnesses of the Resurrection, we cannot overlook the fact that our Lord did not call any women into the circle of disciples and Apostles. The relation of women to Jesus and to his disciples and Apostles lies, on the contrary, in a ministering function of peculiar significance and dignity.

2 *Women distinguished by special activities in the Acts and in the Pauline Epistles*

WHAT function have women in the Christian communities of the Apostolic Age? Apart from the discussions of St. Paul in 1 Cor. 11 and 14, on the fundamentals, we depend on conclusions deduced from occasional references to women in the Pauline Epistles and in the Acts.

The greetings in the Epistle to the Romans are preceded by a commendation of Phoebe, who is called ἀδελφὴ ἡμῶν and διάκονος (Rom. 16:1,2).[11] Whilst the expression ἀδελφὴ ἡμῶν can refer to all women members of the community, διάκονος is a designation of office.[12] What the duties of Phoebe's office of deaconess were can only be a matter of conjecture. Perhaps one clue may be the designation προστάτις.[13] The succour which Phoebe gives to the Apostle and to others is probably a matter of material and administrative assistance.

It is also quite possible that Phoebe gave her services to the poor and the sick of the community. We do not know exactly what her special duty in Rome was.[14] In spite of its lack of clarity, the mention of Phoebe in Romans is sufficient proof of the existence of the office of deaconess in the Apostolic Age, even though no details can be deduced as to the dissemination of the office.[15]

The list of greetings in Romans begins with the names of the Jewish-Christian couple, Prisca[16] and Aquila. That the woman's name is put first gives us the idea that Prisca was more active than her husband, and therefore of more importance.[17] We know of this couple that they had collected around them in Rome a house-church, as they also did in Corinth, when they fled there after the edict of Claudius (Acts 18:1-8).[18] St. Paul owed them especial gratitude, because they 'laid down their own necks' for his life.[19] He calls them συνεργοί μου ἐν Χριστῷ Ἰησοῦ as well, a description which he used for those who helped him in spreading the Gospel.[20] It is not clear of what this help consisted, whether in active participation in preaching or in an indirect way. It is recorded in Acts 18:26 that Priscilla and Aquila 'expounded the way of God more perfectly' to the Alexandrian Jew Apollos in Ephesus. In the preceding verse it is expressly stated that Apollos was 'instructed in the way of the Lord', and correctly taught about Jesus, though he knew only the baptism of John. The activity of Priscilla and Aquila probably consisted in supplementing and deepening the Christian teaching (ὁδός), possibly with special reference to Baptism. It would be an exaggeration to call Priscilla a woman-apostle in this respect.[21] In the expounding to Apollos it is not a question of public proclamation, nor does Priscilla play an official part. The gift of Christian teaching, the power to win members to a house-church, and the help given to the Apostle in his missionary work are to be regarded more as spontaneous expressions of their Christian personality. Priscilla's activity is therefore fundamentally different from Phoebe's office of deaconess, and is exceptional in its individual and unofficial character.

This remark is also valid for the four daughters of Philip the evangelist, 'virgins which did prophesy' (Acts 21:9). The verses following, about the 'prophet named Agabus' who foretold St. Paul's imprisonment at Jerusalem, shows clearly that 'prophesying' here cannot be, as for St. Paul, confined to a speaking by inspiration in church (cf. Acts 13:1), but refers to a foretelling of the future (cf. Acts 11:27). Here it is a foretelling of the future rather than a preaching of the word of God. The mention of the four daughters of Philip is designed to prepare the reader of Acts for the prophecy of Agabus. So there can be no essential difference between the activity of the prophet and that of the prophesying virgins. The prophesying here spoken of is neither a general charismatic phenomenon nor an office based on a special commission, but rather, an individual vocation and gift, having no direct connection with preaching the word in church, and it can thus be bestowed on both men and women.

The greeting in Romans contains other women's names. Mary bestowed much labour on the community (16:6: ἐκοπίασεν). The same expression for corporal or intellectual and spiritual endeavours is used in v. 12 for the work or Tryphena, Tryphosa, and Persis, with the addition ἐν Κυρίῳ, which better describes the work of these women. This cannot refer to an active participation in missionary preaching, for κοπιᾶν is a general expression which always requires a special qualification.[22]

Finally St. Paul, in Phil. 4:2,3, refers to Euodias and Syntyche 'which laboured with me in the Gospel'. As in Rom. 16:6,12, there can be no reference to an official position, or to a participation in preaching. ἐν τῷ εὐαγγελίῳ συναθλεῖν refers to suffering for faith (cf. Phil. 1:27), and is to be understood as the possibility of martyrdom which persists throughout the Epistle to the Philippians.

The examination of all the references in the Pauline Epistles and in Acts therefore shows that women definitely played an active part in the life of the community, without, however, exercising a missionary or teaching office of any kind. Women, whether in official or quasi-official positions, are only found as διάκονοι.

3 *St. Paul's attitude to the position of women in church services*

SO far the picture of women's service in the Hellenistic communities could only be inferred from occasional remarks. St. Paul's fundamental exposition of this theme gives a clearer outline. But before we can discuss 1 Cor. 14:33b-36, we must examine the utterances regarding women's activities in 1 Cor. 11.[23]

In discussing the question of what kind of head-covering the members of the community at Corinth[24] should wear in church, it is assumed that women too can pray and prophesy.[25] This does not refer to any official activity undertaken by particular persons, but to a free, charismatic participation which every man and every woman can exercise.[26] προσεύχεσθαι means 'praying aloud' and προφητεύειν comprehensible speech, in contrast to glossolalia, by inspiration, and the spontaneous proclamation in the Spirit of the divine revelation.[27] That women, in the assembly at Corinth, prayed and prophesied in a charismatic fashion cannot be denied. But it is another question how St. Paul judged these facts. In 1 Cor. 11 he does not adopt any particular attitude. It would be going too far to deduce a special attitude from an incidental remark in v. 5.[28] As St. Paul does not concern himself with this question at all in 1 Cor. 11, we do not know whether, in this case, the praying and prophesying by women in church at Corinth is permitted or disapproved on principle.

But in 1 Cor. 14:33b-36, a thorough discussion and an enunciation of principle occur. The whole of chapter 14 deals with speaking with tongues and prophecy, and with the effectiveness of spiritual gifts in church.[29] After a detailed exposition of the use and order of these gifts in the assembly (vv. 26-33a), St. Paul comes to the activity of women. The immediate taking-up of this question, which apparently interrupts the connection between vv. 33a and 37, and the inversion of vv. 34 and 35 in some MSS,[30] has led to the supposition that a very early interpolation can be found here, based on 1 Tim. 2:11, 12. It has also been suggested that it might be a marginal note by St. Paul himself. But this suggestion is incorrect because in the case of an interpolation, vv. 33b-36 must be regarded as not genuine, as well as vv. 34 and 35, as the MSS referred to would imply. It cannot be seriously maintained that the verses are either not genuine or not in the right place.

The somewhat abrupt passing to a fresh question is probably to be explained by the Apostle's desire to deal at last with the question which he had not yet mentioned in chapter 11, and to speak of women's activities in the assembly. Whilst he merely puts glossolalia within proper bounds, St. Paul absolutely forbids women to speak at all. This command to be silent refers to all ecstatic and edifying speaking, its different possibilities having been enumerated in v. 26. Twice a similar command in a particular case had been given. The speaker with tongues is to be silent if there is no one to interpret (14:28). The prophet is to be silent if a revelation is given to another (14:30). The third prohibition which St. Paul enunciates for the order of the assembly is of a general character and refers to every kind of charismatic speech. In this connection only λαλεῖν is mentioned, not προφητεύειν or διδασκεῖν or ἑρμηνεύειν. Λαλεῖν is not the equivalent of any of these expressions. It embraces all kinds of charismatic utterance. In no circumstances can it refer to a speaking different from that in v. 26.[31] The special nuance of this word lies in its opposition to silence.[32] The assertion of 'another kind of speaking', which St. Paul is here forbidding, cannot be deduced from the use of λαλεῖν.

If we had only this command to be silent to deal with, there would be no question about its meaning. But in v. 35 comes the direction: εἰ δέ τι μαθεῖν θέλουσιν, ἐν οἴκῳ τοὺς ἰδίους ἄνδρας ἐπερωτάτωσαν, the relation of which to the previous command to be silent is of decided significance for the exegesis. For an appropriate interpretation the following alternatives offer themselves: either μαθεῖν interprets the λαλεῖν in v. 34, in which case the prohibition of speech would refer only to intervening questions,[33] or v. 35 intensifies the command to be silent. Women[34] are to be silent as a matter of principle; not even for the sake of μαθεῖν[35] may they speak in the assembly but are to ask their husbands at home.

V. 36 makes it clear that only the second interpretation is suitable.

The polemic rhetorical question as to whether the word of God came *from* the women or only to *them* would have no meaning except for the preceding general command to keep silent, which refers to all charismatic utterance of the word of God by women. If it were an intervening question and discussion, it would hardly have been denoted by ὁ λόγος τοῦ Θεοῦ. [It may be that v. 36 refers rather to the coming of the Gospel from Jerusalem to Corinth, in which case it is possible that λαλεῖν does mean the intervening questions; but if Paul is forbidding even intervening questions, he must *a fortiori* be forbidding extended discourse—Ed.] That the command to be silent in v. 34 is intensified is also obvious from the wider context. As the whole of chapter 14, and especially vv. 33b-36, deals with the ordering of charismatic gifts in church, and that theme is continued in v. 37, it is hardly likely that the intervening vv. 33b-36 should suddenly drop away from the main theme and deal with uncharismatic speaking. Vv. 33b-36 are part and parcel of the whole chapter. Therefore the command to be silent refers, as a matter of principle, to all Spirit-inspired speaking by women in the assembly. The direction to have certain questions answered by their husbands at home only underlines this intensification.

What is the reason for this command to keep silence? In the first place there is the direction ὡς ἐν πάσαις ταῖς ἐκκλησίαις τῶν ἁγίων (33b). St. Paul argued in the same way concerning women's head covering in church: ἡμεῖς τοιαύτην συνήθειαν οὐκ ἔχομεν, οὐδὲ αἱ ἐκκλησίαι τοῦ Θεοῦ. In modern terminology the ecumenical relevance of the problem is at stake. For the sake of the unity of the Church, no contradictory customs and arrangements should be allowed to spring up in the communities (cf. 1 Cor. 4:17; 7:17). A single community which differs from the others on the question of the women's right to proclaim the word of God should, for the sake of unanimity in general practice, be ready to abandon its own customs, for in St. Paul's thought the universal Church has always the priority over the single community. In chapter 11 the argument seems to envisage only the bringing into line of a comparatively unimportant custom. As we shall see below it is here also a question of principle concerning the equality of men and women in church.

The second reason for the command to be silent lies for St. Paul in the νόμος which demands a ὑποτάσσεσθαι of women (14:34). In other places also St. Paul refers to 'the law' for definite directions for community life.[36] He is thinking either of the Pentateuch or also of the rest of the Old Testament.[37] Which passage is St. Paul appealing to in 1 Cor. 14:34? He is still citing Gen. 3:16 (cf. Gen. 18:12), where the headship of the man over the woman is spoken of. True, this passage deals with the submission of the married woman to her husband, whilst the ὑποτάσσεσθαι of 1 Cor. 14:34 is a special kind of principle for the service.[38] But we must not overlook the fact that this special principle of order is founded on the submission of the woman to her husband which, in St. Paul's opinion, goes back to the story of the Fall. It is less likely that St. Paul, by invoking the νόμος, is alluding to the fact that both in ancient Israel and in the Temple and synagogue services of late Judaism, women were excluded from any active participation in the cult. Even on the basis of the argument in 1 Cor. 11, it is more likely that St. Paul starts from the general subordination of women to their husbands, due to the Creation, i.e., the Fall, and goes on to the special principle of order of the ὑποτάσσεσθαι in the assembly.[39]

The motives for the Pauline command to keep silence must be distinguished from the reasons for it. The reference to custom and tradition in the other communities and the abruptness of the diction in 1 Cor. 14:36 show that the Apostle is taking a polemical stand against a bad custom which had grown up in Corinth, and which is, in his eyes, a matter of principle. Behind the behaviour in church of the women of Corinth lies a striving for the principle of the equality of men and women. Considering the inner situation of the Corinthian community, this can only be a matter of putting the ideas of Gnosticism into practice.[40] According to the Gnostic Redemption-myth there can be no more difference between the sexes. The particles of primal man can find a habitation in either a masculine or a feminine σάρξ. In the πνεῦμα all natural and created features are abolished.[41] We also know that in the Gnostic conventicles could be seen the practical consequences of the fundamental equality of men and women.[42] The community of Corinth was under the influence of these Gnostic ideas, and tried to put them into practice in its services. This is the real position which St. Paul is attacking. Lastly, it is not for him a matter of this or that custom, but a yes or no to an elementary *theologumenon* of Gnosticism. If we consider this polemical goal of Pauline argument, then these two reasons for the command to women to keep silence stand out even more clearly. The postulate of the unity of the Church in the ordering of services and the idea that the sexes are unequal by Creation stand in complete opposition to the theory and practice of Gnosticism, and are, at the same time, decisive reasons for the impossibility of associating the Corinthian custom with general church order.

These two anti-gnostic arguments are also found in 1 Cor. 11, where the head-covering of women in church is in question.[43] Here St. Paul turns against the Gnostic equalisation of men and women. The reference to the custom in other communities (11:16) is, again, not in isolation. The difference of the sexes is established by the Apostle in two ways. He first speaks of the κεφαλή-ship of the man. Whatever conception St. Paul expressed by the idea of κεφαλή,[44] he wishes, by the gradation God/Christ/Man/Woman (11:3), to prevent the false equalising of the sexes, without expressing thereby a creaturely inferiority of woman to man. More persuasive is the Apostle's demonstration in 11:8,9. He is dealing with an interpretation of the Creation-story in Gen. 2:8ff, which excludes the equality of the sexes. The man is εἰκών and δόξα of God (11:1), ἡ γυνὴ δὲ δόξα ἀνδρὸς ἐστιν. The order of creation is emphasised: γυνὴ ἐξ ἀνδρός (11:8), and finally the woman was created for the sake of the man (11:9). St. Paul is only concerned to oppose a Gnostic emancipation of women. It would be drawing a wrong conclusion to demonstrate from his arguments that he considered women to be religiously and essentially inferior. St. Paul wants to prevent such a false interpretation of his argument, and therefore adds: 'Nevertheless neither is the man without the woman, neither the woman without the man, in the Lord. For as the woman is of the man, even so is the man also by the woman; but all things of God' (11:11,12). If he did first insist on the created differences of the sexes in his anti-gnostic attitude, yet it would be a misunderstanding if an absolute difference were deduced from this, for ἐν Κυρίῳ this difference between man and woman is abolished and only the principle τὰ δὲ πάντα ἐκ τοῦ Θεοῦ counts.

In the Epistle to the Galatians St. Paul uses Gnostic notions to express the fundamental equality of man and woman. 'There is neither Jew nor Greek, there is neither bond nor free, there is neither male nor female: for ye are all one in Christ' (Gal. 3:28). In v. 27 the reason for this unity is said to be in Christ: 'For as many of you as have been baptised into Christ, have put on Christ'. For the old differences of religious and social origins, as well as the sexes, have been annulled in those who have received the sacrament of Baptism.[45] Man and woman are now a unity ἐν Χριστῷ Ἰησοῦ, whose members they have become in Baptism. Their natural individuality has been taken up into the totality of the σῶμα Χριστοῦ, into which they have been integrated by the sacrament.

However much St. Paul represents this view, couched in Gnostic terms, of the sacramental-ontological equality of all the baptised as members of Christ's body, he yet decisively, on the other hand, opposes an equality of the sexes which disregards the natural order of Creation. For the Apostle there is a sharply-drawn frontier between the positive assimilation of Gnostic ideas and the clear rejection of the same ideas in the case of their incompatibility with the Christian idea of Creation. St. Paul finds no direct practical inferences from the sacramental reality of the Body of Christ for the ordering of the assembly and its services. The decisive rejection of an equalisation of men and women in the concrete situations of 1 Cor. 11 and 14 is the more weighty in the face of the *theologumenon* of a fundamental equality of the sexes represented in 1 Cor. 11:11,12 and Gal. 3:28. Was St. Paul inconsistent? Did he let himself be led astray by his anti-gnostic polemic to make the principle of the equality of the sexes relative, or even to abolish it, in 1 Cor. 11 and 14? Can the Apostle's command to keep silence be discounted by the Church, since it arose out of a particular polemical situation, in contrast to his original insight? But it is not suitable to make St. Paul's different views relative, or to play off one against the other.⁴⁶ The duty of every serious interpretation is to seek after the complementary meaning of such differing statements without becoming involved in the search for a false harmonisation. Both the sentences about the equality and inequality of the sexes are therefore to be understood not only in their temporal but also in their fundamental theological meaning. The difference between man and woman arising from Creation, and the sacramental unity and equality originating from Redemption, are not contradictory, nor do they cancel each other out. The recourse to the order of Creation is in no way a concession to anti-gnostic polemic, but it corresponds absolutely to the fundamental theological insight that the circumstances of Creation have been transformed sacramentally by Redemption, though they are still valid for the concrete ordering of the community. The complete negation of the theological relevance of the reality of Creation on the Gnostic side and the resulting practical consequence were for St. Paul an immediate impulse to his insight and decision that in Christian worship men only were to be called to the various offices of proclaiming the word. So it cannot be doubted that St. Paul, with his apostolic authority, has given a decision, in his command to women to keep silence, which is still binding on the Church of today.

4 *The duties of women according to the Pastoral Epistles*

SOME decades after St. Paul we find in the pseudo-Pauline Pastoral Epistles a further discussion of the place of women. 1 Tim. 2:8-15 deals with a kind of regulation for the community concerning the behaviour of men and women in church.⁴⁷ Contrasted with 1 Cor. 14:33b-36, this passage shows an intensification: 'Let the woman learn in silence with all subjection. But I suffer not a woman to teach, nor to usurp authority over the man, but to be in silence' (1 Tim. 2, 11, 12). As in 1 Cor. 14:35, the matter is that of learning in connection with the preaching of the word. But whereas in 1 Cor. 14:35 the woman is recommended to converse with her husband at home, 1 Tim. 2 mentions only the possibility of learning quietly at home in all subjection. The woman must submit to the regulations for the assembly and must receive the preaching of the men without interfering with questions. The ἐν ἡσυχίᾳ μανθάνειν corresponds to the command to keep silence, the ἐν πάσῃ ὑποταγῇ to the ὑποτάσσεσθαι of 1 Cor. 14:34. 1 Tim. 2:13 shows that a subjection of the woman to the man is meant, the origin of which lies in the Creation of man, and which has practical results for behaviour in church. The generally disseminated *paraenesis* of the subjection of the woman to the man⁴⁸ is here taken up and applied to the conditions of the assembly. In contrast to 1 Cor. 14, the command to be silent is now made more precise by an explicit prohibition of teaching: διδάσκειν δὲ γυναικί οὐκ ἐπιτρέπω (2:12). διδάσκειν cannot refer to charismatic speaking, but to official teaching in the assembly. Because the Pastoral Epistles do not, as does 1 Cor. 14, deal with the exercise of free personal charisma, but with the preaching of the word legitimised by ecclesiastical authority,[49] the mere command to keep silence must be replaced by an express prohibition to teach. The writer of 1 Tim. seems to be in a polemical situation when he forbids a woman to desire lordship over the man. The αὐθεντεῖν ἀνδρός is too subtle a controversial formulation, and is directed against a Gnostic equalisation of men and women in church. Possibly there is an allusion to the pretensions of 'charismatic' women to taking precedence of the official teachers and to a tendency to interrupt.[50] The anti-gnostic polemic is made particularly clear by the recommendation of τεκνογονία as the duty suitable to woman (2:15; cf. 5:14). This high estimation of childbearing is joined with a condemnation of a Gnostic asceticism grounded in mythology (cf. 1 Tim. 4:3). Thus here also there is a likeness between 1 Cor. 14 and the regulations of the Pastoral Epistles, just as the εἶναι ἐν ἡσυχίᾳ (2:12) corresponds to St. Paul's command to keep silence. The reason given in v. 13 for the subjection of the woman, that Adam was created before Eve, coincides with the Pauline way of thought of 1 Cor. 11:7-9, which also lies behind the notion of subjection in 1 Cor. 14:34. The second reason, given in v. 14, that it was Eve, and not Adam, who was tempted, does not occur in St. Paul, although the idea of the women's proneness to temptation is not foreign to him (2 Cor. 11:3). Whether this coincidence of both terminology and subject matter is due to the imitation of the Pauline example (this would explain the pseudonymous character of the Epistle), or whether this comes from a tradition of teaching influenced by St. Paul, cannot as yet be definitely decided. But the pertinent correspondence is not in doubt. In his directions concerning the ordering of the gifts of the Spirit in the assembly St. Paul emphasised his apostolic authority,[51] and the commands in 1 Tim. concerning the behaviour of men and women in church are also grounded on such an authority. The conscious and decisive desire of the Apostle is meant to be expressed by βούλομαι (2:8) and ἐπιτρέπω (2:12).[52] The ordering, which includes the prohibition to women to teach, is therefore not only bound up with a temporal situation, but is rather to be regarded as generally binding and valid for the life of the Church.[53] The formal claim, which the Pastoral Epistles make, in their pseudepigraphic dress, receives its corroboration by its pertinent conformity with the teachings of the Apostle Paul.

Besides the prohibition to teach, the Pastoral Epistles also contain references to the fact that women exercised certain functions in the community. 1 Tim. 5:9 refers to widows who are to be 'taken into the number'. The condition for being thus 'taken into the number' is fulfilled by a widow who is not 'under threescore years old, having been the wife of one man, well-reported of for good works; if she have brought up children, if she have lodged strangers, if she have washed the saints' feet, if she have relieved the afflicted, if she have diligently followed every good work' (5:9,10).[54] It cannot be definitely decided whether this refers only to the condition of widowhood in general, or to a regular office of widow with defined duties and rights. What is striking is that some of the activities here listed could well belong to the sphere of a deaconess such as Phoebe, mentioned in Rom. 16:1. But a regulated and organised charitable activity in a particular condition of life does not necessarily mean that all widows who have been 'taken into the number' administered an office, in the specialised meaning of the word.

5 *The actual authority of the New Testament statements concerning the services and duties of women in the community*

THUS the witness of the New Testament gives us a clear and homogeneous picture of the office held by women in the Christian community. As in the life of Jesus, women in primitive Christianity also exercised functions of service. The office of deaconess gave expression to the special gifts and duties of women. But women are not allowed the office of preaching (and that would naturally include administration of the sacraments), whether in a free, charismatic or a specific, official form. This is not a matter of accidental, temporary character, due to the position of women in the classical world of primitive Christianity; it is a deliberate decision. Though this decision was arrived at in a particular controversial situation, it is meant as a permanent principle. As it rests on the highest authority possible in the Church, i.e., Apostolic authority, this decision must be equally valid and binding for the Church of the present day.[55] The recognition of the Apostolic command to keep silence and to refrain from teaching in the assembly should be not merely an act of obedience to Apostolic authority, but also the recognition of the theological reasons for this command. For both the reasons given by the Apostle Paul are of actual significance and validity. He who sees the unity of the Church as the goal and standard for ecclesiastical work, and who recognises the relationship between the order of Creation and that of Redemption correctly (i.e., according to the Apostles) must regard the command to women to keep silence and to refrain from teaching in the assembly as still valid and binding for today.

NOTES

[1] cf., e.g., Mark 5:21ff, the healing of the woman with an issue of blood and the raising of Jairus's daughter; Mark 7:24ff, the healing of the Syro-Phoenician woman's daughter; John 4:1ff, the woman of Samaria; Luke 10:38ff, Martha and Mary; Luke 7:36ff, the anointing by the woman that was a sinner; Mark 14:3ff, the anointing by the woman of Bethany. In general cf. J. Leipholdt, *Jesus und die Frauen*, 1921, and *Die Frau in der antiken Welt und im Urchristentum*, 2nd ed., 1955.

[2] cf., Luke 23:49,55, the reference to 'the women who followed him from Galilee'.

[3] Luke names Mary Magdalene, Joanna, and Susanna (8:2ff); Mary Magdalene, Joanna, Mary the mother of James (24:10); Mark names Mary Magdalene, Mary the mother of James, and Salome (15:40). The discrepancy amongst the lists of names is due to the fact that in oral tradition, names are easily changed about. A comparison of Luke with Mark reveals that (i) Mary Magdalene held the most important place amongst the women; (ii) the circle of women who followed Jesus in Galilee and ministered to him is fundamentally the same as the group mentioned in Luke 8:2,3.

[4] Tabitha is described in Acts 9:36 as μαθήτρια. It is said of her, 'this woman was full of good works and almsdeeds which she did'. We find here an unqualified expression. In Acts the Christians are generally referred to as 'disciples', cf., e.g., 6:1,7; 9:19. In the technical meaning of the word, Mary is spoken of as a μαθήτρια τοῦ Κυρίου in the apocryphal Gospel of Peter (15:20).

[5] This is specially underlined in Luke 8:2.

[6] cf., Mark 15:47; Matt. 27:61; Luke 23:55.

[7] cf., Mark 16:3; Matt. 28:1ff; Luke 24:2; John 20:1.

[8] cf., Mark 16:5; Matt. 28:9; Luke 24:4.

[9] cf., Mark 16:7; Matt. 28:8; Luke 24:9; John 20:18.

[10] cf., Mark 16:9ff; John 20:11ff.

[11] For exegetical details cf. the respective commentaries, esp. O. Michel, *Der Brief an die Römer*, 1955.

[12] This is obvious from the preceding participle οὖσαν and the genitive following, τῆς ἐκκλησίας τῆς ἐν Κενχρεαῖς.

[13] προστάτις can, like the masculine form προστάτης, be a reference to office, but here the word is probably used in its general meaning. cf., the parallels in the dictionaries.

[14] Perhaps it was she who delivered the Epistle. Her duty in Rome seems to be referred to in Rom. 16:2. πρᾶγμα can refer to a legal matter (cf., 1 Cor. 6:1). The usual meaning of the word, 'affair, business', is here to be preferred.

[15] Whether 1 Tim. 3:11 refers to deaconesses is doubtful. Probably the reference is to the wives of deacons.

[16] The diminutive of this name is Priscilla. cf., Acts 18:18,26.
[17] 2 Tim. 4:19 seems to follow the Pauline example in a pseudepigraphic manner, but also in Acts 18:18,26, Priscilla is named first. However, in 1 Cor. 16:19 the order is reversed.
[18] cf., Rom. 16:3 and 1 Cor. 16:9. House-churches under the leadership of women are attested elsewhere. In Col. 4:16, greetings are sent to Nymphe and the church in her house.
[19] cf., Rom. 16:4. Where this took place is not known. Perhaps in Ephesus, cf., Acts 19:23.
[20] e.g. Rom. 16:9,21; Phil. 2:25; Philemon 1,24.
[21] as does Harnack, *Die Mission und Ausbreitung des Christentums in den ersten drei Jahrhunderten*, 4th ed., 1924, p. 593.
[22] e.g. in 1 Tim. 5:17.
[23] cf., Else Kähler, *Die Frau in den paulinischen Briefen unter besonderer Berücksichtigung des Begriffes der Unterordnung*, 1960, where all previous literature is summed up in an exemplary fashion. Otherwise we need only cite H. Lietzman-W. C. Kummel, *An die Korinther I/II, Handbuch zum Neuen Testament*, 1949, W. Schmithals, *Die Gnosis in Korinth*, 1956, and G. Fitzer, '*Das Weib schweige in der Gemeinde*'. *Uber den unpaulinschen Chararkter der mulier taceat-Verse in I Korinther xiv*, 1963.
[24] That this should refer only to a house-church assembly is impossible in face of the discussion of the Eucharistic service which follows in 11:17ff.
[25] 1 Cor. 11:5: Πᾶσα δὲ γυνὴ προσευχομένη ἢ προφητεύουσα. Cf. v. 13, which refers only to women praying.
[26] 1 Cor. 11:4: πᾶς ἀνήρ ... 11:5 πᾶσα δὲ γυνή ... πᾶς, πᾶσα testifies that no further qualification is necessary.
[27] cf., 1 Cor. 13:9; 14:1,3-5,24,31,39; Matt. 7:22; Acts 2:17; 19:6; 21:9, Rev. 11:3.
[28] St. Paul proceeds in the same way in 1 Cor. 15:29, in dealing with vicarious Baptism. The mention of the prevailing custom of Baptism for the dead is here used in the special argumentation, cf., chap. 15. But that does not by any means imply that the Apostle approves of the custom. The contrary is more probable.
[29] cf., the enumeration is v. 26: ψαλμός, διδαχή, ἀποκάλυψις, λαλεῖν ἐν γλώσσῃ, ἑρμηνεία. The meaning and goal of all charismatic activity is summed up in the sentence: πάντα πρὸς οἰκοδόμην γενέσθω.
[30] The vv. 34,35 are placed at the end of the chapter in the MSS DG 88 it and in Ambrosiaster.
[31] This is against Kähler, *op. cit.*, p. 77, who espouses the opinion, without evidence, that λαλεῖν could not include any προφητεύειν. The use of the word in 1 Cor. 14:6 in connection with γλῶσσα, ἀποκάλυψις, γνῶσις, προφητεία, διδαχή makes this assertion impossible (cf., 14:27, 28,29). True, λαλεῖν can mean chatter (cf., 1 Cor. 13:11; 1 Tim. 5:13), but a positive meaning is much more frequent, e.g. Rom. 7:1;

1 Cor. 15:34; 2 Cor. 13:3. In Rom. 3:19 and 1 Cor. 9:8 λαλεῖν and λέγειν are used synonymously.

[32] cf., e.g. Mark 1:34; Luke 4:41; Acts 18:9.

[33] cf., Kähler, *op. cit.*, p. 76: 'In the situation considered by St. Paul the prophesying woman is not in question. St. Paul deals only with the 'speaking' woman (λαλεῖν) who disturbs the service and who is therefore commanded to be silent.'

[34] St. Paul is thinking chiefly of married women, who probably formed the majority of the community. Unmarried women naturally come under the same principle.

[35] Probably μαθεῖν is not to be equated with the charismatic διερμηνεύειν in v. 27 and the διακρίνειν of v. 29. It is more likely to be a matter of questions and discussion following the interpretation of glossolalia and prophecy.

[36] cf., 1 Cor. 9:8ff; 14:21. Concerning St. Paul's use of language, cf., the article νόμος in *Theologisches Wörterbuch* (ed. Kittel), Vol. IV, pp. 1062f.; 1070.

[37] In 1 Cor. 9:8 the quotation is Deut. 25:4 and in 1 Cor. 14:21 it is Isa. 28:11b and Deut. 28:49.

[38] This is specially brought out by Kähler, *op. cit.*, p. 82.

[39] This principle of subordination also disposes of the objection that St. Paul could not have opposed the gifts of the Spirit (1 Thess. 5:19,20).

[40] cf., Schmithals, *op. cit.*, pp. 207-209. The hypothesis that 1 Cor. 11 and 14 come from different Epistles, and that this results in different views on the question of women, cannot be substantiated.

[41] cf., as the best example the notice from the Egyptian Gospel by Clement of Alexandria, Strom. III. 99ff. (ed. Stahlin, 238, 22ff.): 'Said the Lord: "If ye tread the robe of shame underfoot, and if two become one, the masculine with the feminine [will be] neither masculine nor feminine".' In this respect we should also remember the Gnostic preference for masculine-feminine primal beings. cf., the last logion of the Gnostic Gospel of Thomas!

[42] cf., e.g., the description of the prophetesses of Marcus in Irenaeus. *Adv. Haer.* 1.13.3.

[43] For all exegetic details, cf., Kähler, *op. cit.*, pp. 43ff, and Schmithals, *op. cit.*, pp. 201-207.

[44] cf., the excursus in Kähler, *op. cit.* pp. 47ff.

[45] Similar enumerations in connection with Baptism can be found in 1 Cor. 12:13, and Col. 3:11. In both cases, however, the apposite pair is missing, ἄρσεν καὶ θῆλυ.

[46] Here we are in opposition to Schmithal's argument, *op. cit.*, pp. 230ff, where he makes one idea of the Apostle's into a temporary polemic, for the benefit of another.

[47] For all exegetical details cf. Kähler, *op. cit.*, pp. 147ff, and M. Dibelius

and H. Conzelmann, *Die Pastoralbriefe, Handbuch zum Neuen Testament* 13, 1955, ad loc.

[48] cf., Col. 3:18; Eph. 5:22,29; 1 Peter 3:1,5; Titus 2:5; here the purpose of the subjection is seen in 'that the word of God be not blasphemed.'

[49] cf., the ordination of Timothy, 1 Tim. 4:14; 2 Tim. 1:6. For the 'character of office' in the Pastoral Epistles, cf. Kähler, *op. cit.*, p. 145.

[50] cf., the translation and commentary by Dibelius and Conzelmann, *op. cit., ad loc.*

[51] cf., 1 Cor. 14:37; ἃ γράφω ὑμῖν ὅτι Κυρίου ἐστιν ἐντολή.

[52] For βούλομαι in 2:8, cf., 1 Tim. 5:14 and Titus 3:8.

[53] Kähler, *op. cit.*, p. 160, denies this claim, because, together with some other theologians, she believes that certain statements in the Pastoral Epistles should be placed in the periphery of the Canon. That in such a proceeding the theological prejudices of the commentator play a decisive part is obvious.

[54] Titus 2:4,5 sees the chief duties of the widows to be the education of younger women for marriage and family life. Charitable duties are not mentioned.

[55] As to the fundamental question of the validity of an Apostolic decision, cf., H. von Campenhausen, *Die Begründung kirchlicher Entscheidung beim Apostel Paulus*, Heidelberg, 1957.

[*Note*. This essay was first published in German, in *Novum Testamentum*, VII, 2, 1964. It now appears in English with acknowledgments to its original publisher, E. J. Brill of Leiden.]

Representative Priesthood ?

J. I. PACKER

GOOD wine needs no bush, nor do good causes need bad arguments. Bad arguments, indeed, will make their goodness suspect. Whether ordaining women to the presbyterate is a good cause or not may here be left open, but it is certainly daunting to see how often arguments in favour of this practice turn out to be bad ones. A case in point is the line of argument expressed in recent years as follows (my italics):

'We are convinced that the Church needs without delay a *representative* ministry of women just as it needs a *representative* priesthood of men' (*Gender & Ministry*, CIO, 1962, p. 17).

'The ordained ministry is *representative* of Jesus Christ in the Church and of the whole Church which is His Body. . . . Since he *represents* both men and women the ordained ministry ought surely to be composed of both. Can it be truly *representative* of the whole Church if it does not comprise both sexes? Is there not a sense in which the present three-fold ministry is "defective" or "lame" because it excludes the characteristics, qualities and experience which women would bring?' (*Women & Holy Orders*, Anglican Group for the Ordination of Women to the Historic Ministry of the Church, n.d., p. 2).

'A woman's priesthood, it is true, would not be the same as a man's. But women would bring to the priesthood particular gifts and insights which would enlarge its scope, enrich its witness and make it truly *representative*' (*Women & Holy Orders*, CIO, 1966, p. 29).

In this argument, which turns on the idea of the ministerial priest as a representative person, two assumptions are involved.

1. It is assumed that presbyteral priesthood is a form of ministry which involves a representative relationship (a double one, in fact, as we shall see) operating at two distinct levels. In addition to being the appointed delegate of the parties represented, the priest (so it is being assumed) ought as far as possible to exhibit the personal qualities of those parties, and so be a sample as well as a spokesman. Now it is true that the words 'representative' and 'represent' can be used in either of these senses separately, as when a political leader is said to represent those for whom he speaks irrespective of character-differences

between him and them, or when Dr. Billy Graham is said to represent a whole class of American evangelists inasmuch as they are like him and he like them. But when it is assumed that Christian presbyters must represent the Church in both senses at once the question arises whether this is an insight or a confusion, and in the absence of scriptural argument for the former it is hard to avoid concluding the latter.[1]

2. It is also assumed that as priests are representative persons in this double sense, so they represent two distinct parties to each other: God in Christ to the Church, and the Church to him. This is not controversial: the Ordinal tells presbyters to preach, teach, declare forgiveness and shepherd the flock in the Lord's name, and the liturgy tells them to address God in the congregation's name (and it is inevitable, just as it is regrettable, that the world judges the Church by its clergy). But why should this ministerial representation of the Lord and the Church to each other be held to necessitate that some priests be women? Such necessity seems neither logical nor theological (i.e., biblically determined). Perhaps what is in the minds of those who call the all-male Anglican ministry 'defective' and 'lame' is that whereas the presbyter's ministry involves the showing of pastoral sympathy (as did that of the Jewish High Priests, and as does that of the Lord Jesus: see Heb. 4:14-5:2), men and women differ so much that men cannot appreciate or minister to women's problems. Experience, however, down the centuries testifies otherwise; the supposition is as false as it would be to assume that Christ, being sinless, cannot feel for and with sinners.

The idea that the ministry represents the church has been an Anglican commonplace since R. C. Moberly's *Ministerial Priesthood* appeared in 1897—'still' according to Professor A. T. Hanson in 1969 'the best single work written by an Anglican' on its subject.[2] Moberly's contention is that the Christian presbyterate and episcopate are priestly by virtue of being the church's appointed organ for the liturgical fulfilment of its corporate priesthood in Christ. A liberal catholic, steering between the view that priestly ministry in the apostolic succession is constitutive of the Church and the view that there is nothing specially priestly about the Christian ministry at all, Moberly argued three positions: first, that the total Church is priestly because its life in Christ is one of loving self-offering to God and man, as Christ's own life was and is; second, that this life-activity requires external liturgical expression (supremely in the eucharist); third, that ordained clergy are the authorised and empowered agents who 'represent, act for, and wield ministerially the powers of the whole', and who as individuals may properly be called priests because they embody 'with an eminent distinctiveness' the 'concentrated meaning' of the Church's priesthood.[3] But Moberly's line of argument, even if accepted in its entirety, does not bear on the point at issue, which is whether the existing ministry is 'lame' for lack of women. Moberly is arguing that what is concentrated in ministerial priests is the Church's priestly calling, not its bisexuality as a human community nor its corporate experience of grace; his line of thought does not touch the question of women in the ministry, and it contains nothing to counter the observations that 'a male priest represents both sexes in a way which a woman does not, in organised society and church', and 'men and women on the whole will not value women as representatives; they estimate women in their own personal right'.[4] The very existence of Women's Lib. shows that these observations are true as a matter of fact, and public reaction to the movement suggests that they are likely to remain so.

Indeed, if sexual correspondence is held to be required for truly representative ministry the argument for an all-male clergy because of the maleness of Christ (the emblem of his masterfulness as our Saviour) is much stronger than the argument for a bisexual clergy because the Church is bisexual, if only because the minister's representative relations to Christ, as his ambassador, is in every way prior to his relation to the Church, as its liturgical agent. C. S. Lewis argued that a Church which ordains women becomes 'less like a church' because its order then witnesses a degree less clearly to the spiritual reality which makes the Church, namely the lordly saving ministry of Christ himself. In the army, wrote Lewis, 'you salute the uniform, not the wearer. Only one wearing the masculine uniform can (provisionally, and till the Parousia) represent the Lord to the Church; for we are all, corporately and individually, feminine to him.'[5] In the orders of both creation and redemption, what man is to woman is an emblem of what God is to us all: 'we are dealing with male and female not merely as facts of nature but as live and awful shadows of realities utterly beyond our control are largely beyond our direct knowledge;'[6] and where our knowledge lacks fulness as it does here we are in no position to innovate. It is hard to counter reasoning like this from any Christian standpoint, and from the standpoint of the argument under review impossible.

We conclude, then, that the particular argument which we set ourselves to examine is intrinsically unconvincing, boomerangs, and so tends to discredit its own cause.

Notes

[1] As does V. A. Demant when he speaks of the sentence quoted above from *Gender & Ministry* as containing 'a confusion between representation as meaning likeness of the specimen to the things represented, and representation as a deputed delegative function' (*Women & Holy Orders*, p. 110).
[2] Introduction to SPCK reprint, 1969, p. xviii.
[3] Moberly, *op. cit.*, pp. 259-262. Moberly's view, though widely accepted, can be criticised as (a) giving precedence to a function (priesthood in the church's name) which the New Testament nowhere explicitly mentions (b) not giving precedence to the functions of preaching, teaching and ruling in Christ's name which are central in the New Testament account of the Christian ministry (c) assimilating the Church's priesthood too closely to Christ's High Priesthood. The remarkable influence which Moberly's view has had may reflect less its intrinsic cogency and scripturalness than its attraction as a counterweight to Roman views and its strong moral appeal to an institutionalised body of clergymen.
[4] Demant, *op. cit.*, pp. 110, 111. [5] *Undeceptions*, Bles, 1971, p. 195. [6] *op. cit.*, p. 196.

Demythologising the Liberal Illusion

HANS C. CAVALLIN

THE TITLE of this essay may sound rather provocative. It is not our aim, however, to try to prove that Liberalism as a political, economic or philosophical doctrine is an illusion, nor are we going to demythologise Liberal ideas about women as such. Here we are only concerned with the contention that these Liberal ideas are to be found in the Bible, the New Testament or the teaching of Jesus. Is that contention correct or is it an illusion? That is the thrust of this investigation.

Generally speaking, Liberal ideas about the position of the woman in the family and in the community have been accepted by modern civilisation. The Convention of the United Nations on the political rights of women gives a very clear expression to these ideas. The Convention states that 'women shall be entitled to hold public offices and to exercise all public functions established by national law, on equal terms with men, without any discrimination'.[1] The keyword of the modern view on the relation between men and women is *equality*, one of the three watchwords of the French Revolution in 1789. The aim of the movement for the emancipation of women was to establish equality between men and women as far as possible. This movement towards equality has above all been an assimilation of women towards men, not *vice versa*. Women have taken positions, which could earlier have been held only by men. But, as a result of this development, men, to some extent, have been obliged to do things which they never used to do, such as washing up, caring for young children, etc. Physiological facts are the only limit to this process of assimilation. This frontier has not yet been crossed even in the *kibbutzim* of modern Israel, where equality between men and women is worked out more uncompromisingly than in most other modern communities. But in all fields of community life, where physiological facts do not play the most important part, Liberalism and much modern opinion affirm a total equality and likeness between men and women. From this point of view, the ordination of women to the priesthood is a matter of course. But may one change a two thousand year old tradition in the Church just by referring to modern views? The accommodation of the practice and teaching of Christianity to one's own time cannot be a matter of course. It has to be proved that such accommodation does not change anything essential in Christianity. Is the ordination of women to the priesthood, a matter of inevitability to Liberalism and much modern opinion, in accordance with the teaching of the Bible, the New Testament or Jesus of Nazareth concerning the nature of woman and the nature of priesthood? Here we concentrate on the first part of this question. Those who answer it in the affirmative state that the teaching of the Bible and the New Testament on woman, is essentially the same as the corresponding Liberal and modern understanding, or at least similar to it.

This question is only part of the greater question about the relation between modern thinking, influenced by Liberal ideas, and the Bible, the New Testament and the teaching of Jesus. It is well known that about fifty years ago this question was answered by leading Protestant theologians roughly in this way:

> The Liberal religion of Humanism was the teaching of the historic Jesus; it forms the climax of a religious-ethical evolution from the primitive naturalistic religion of old Israel to the high ethical ideals and severe monotheism of the prophets, which were choked by the Law-theology of post-exilic Judaism; Jesus brings religion back to its fresh well-springs; the core of this teaching is trust in the heavenly Father and the unselfish love of the neighbour; after Jesus, his disciples relapse partly into Judaism, and partly into Hellenistic religious thought; thus, for the Gospel of Jesus about the Father and his Kingdom, Paul substitutes his own Gospel about Jesus Christ, as the Son of God, a Saviour who died and rose again; so the disciples of Jesus re-edit his message according to their misunderstanding of it and put words in his mouth, which are clearly not genuine, since they do not agree with the picture of Jesus that the Liberals thought they were able to reconstruct, that picture which so very well corresponded to the religious and ethical ideals of the time.

People at that time had such a reverence for Jesus that they could not believe that he was anything other than they wanted the greatest of the sons of mankind to be. There is a moving apologetic zeal in this more or less unconscious accommodation of Jesus to the highest ideals of the time. Yet it is now almost an axiom of theology that this way of getting at the historic Jesus is untenable from a scholarly point of view. That does not alter the fact that the way in which 'Liberal theology' looks at Jesus and the Bible still plays an influential part, not only in popular discussions, where it is still predominant, but also among many professional theologians, although these often seek to deny it. The leading feature of Liberal theology's reading of the biblical texts was its selectively critical principle, the presupposition of which was nothing else than the Liberal ideals themselves. That which agreed with them, or could be interpreted in accordance with them, was genuinely prophetic or a genuine word of Jesus. Everything else was primitive religion, post-exilic Jewish legalism or *Gemeindetheo-*

logie. It was the *religionsgeschichtliche Schule,* as is well known, which started undermining this manner of interpreting the Bible. The apologetic tendency yielded to more objectively descriptive science. Instead of a 'simple teaching of Jesus', there were now found in the words of Jesus according to the Gospels very primitive, though to modern people strange, Jewish thoughts about the speedy destruction of the world and about what was to happen in this connection. Jesus, who had earlier been so close to modern Western man, was thus moved far away in an Oriental mythical twilight. The resultant conceptions of Jesus proved to have very few things in common with enlightened modern thinking. During the last decades exegesis has gone further in this direction. The Liberal illusion about the simple teaching of Jesus is now generally discredited.[2] After the first period of the *religionsgeschichtliche Schule* (Reitzenstein, Wetter and others), when enthusiasm for parallels between the New Testament and Hellenistic mystery-religions flourished almost without limit, a more sober approach to New Testament exegesis has set in. Now scholars attempt to analyse the thinking of the New Testament objectively, without removing that which does not agree with their own world-picture. (It is another question, of course, whether they always succeed). These are well known facts of the history of theology.[3] Our intention is to try to find an answer to our question about the relation between Liberal and biblical views on woman, according to these principles of 'realistic Bible research' (the slogan of Anton Fridrichsen), and of an 'immanent study of the New Testament' (the watchword of Hugo Odeberg). Are those people right, who want to find the Liberal view of woman in the Bible? Or have they worked according to a selective principle, previously determined (but seldom exactly defined), so that they have been able to unearth ideas which agree with their views on woman, and which are found in certain strata of the biblical material, and on the basis of which they can commend the ordination of women to the priesthood as possible or even desirable?

We need to investigate the texts which are quoted by those who want to find support for Liberal views about woman within the Bible.

1. *The Old Testament*

WE start with the Creation story, Gen. 1: 27: 'So God created man in his own image, in the image of God created he him; male and female created he them'. This passage plays a decisive part in Miss Thrall's *The Ordination of Women to the Priesthood* (1958).[4] She asserts that the difference with regard to the view on woman between Gen. 1 and Gen. 2 is 'absolutely fundamental'.[5] In the Creation story of Gen. 2 the woman's equality of being the image of God is only secondary, mediated through the man, as it is also seen by St. Paul in 1 Cor. 11: 3ff.

Consequently, according to Gen. 2, the woman has to be subordinate to the man. In Gen. 1, on the other hand, nothing is said about the subordination of the woman to the man. On the contrary, according to Gen. 1, both man and woman are created in the image of God, so that 'according to Genesis 1, men and women, created alike in the Image of God, owe an equal and independent obedience to their Creator, and are possessed of an equal authority over the rest of creation. Nothing is said about the subjection of one sex to the other, so that we cannot assume it to be a general principle that either should be subordinate'.[6] This interpretation of Gen. 1: 27 finds an apparent fulfilment in the New Testament: (a) 'The work of Christ is the complete realisation of man's existence in the Image of God. Therefore he fulfils the conception of the ideal man as it is presented to us in Genesis 1. (b) Through the work of Christ, the woman no less than the man, is able to grow into the kind of existence postulated for her in the Genesis 1 story. (c) Therefore the woman achieves an independent relationship with God in which Christ is the only intermediary.'[7] Miss Thrall is not content just to establish a contrast between Gen. 1: 27 and 2: 21f, 3: 16 and passages in the New Testament dependent on these. She wants also to give a harmonising explanation of this contrast.[8] The subordination according to Gen. 2: 21f, 3: 16, 1 Cor. 11: 3f, 14: 34f, Eph. 5: 22f, Col. 3: 18f, and other passages is only to be regarded as a temporary stage for the woman, necessary before she can reach the full equality with the man as expressed in Gen. 1: 27, and according to 'the wider implications of New Testament theology in respect of the theological status of the woman'.[9]

Miss Thrall makes considerable efforts to do justice to everything the biblical texts tell us about the relation between men and women. But the whole of her interesting description of the biblical view on woman stands or falls by her interpretation of the relation between the first and the second Creation story with regard to the creation of man. One has to point out that this interpretation is essentially an argument from silence. 'In Genesis 1 there is no mention whatsoever of the subordination of the woman to the man,' it is said on the decisive point[10] (which is of course correct, if you do not emphasise the fact that 'male' is mentioned before 'female'). The statement that the description in Gen. 2 of the relation between man and woman is only a 'stage in the growth of human personality into the complete Image of the Creator'[11] lacks every foundation in the texts. Miss Thrall constructs a disjunction between Gen. 1: 27 and 2: 21f, on the basis of (to say the least) a debatable interpretation of the texts, but it would be most natural to regard the latter description of the relation between man and woman as a complement of the former. Gen. 1: 27 does not say anything at all more exactly about the relation between 'male' and 'female', at least absolutely nothing about the woman as enjoying 'an independent existence in the Image, an existence which she possesses, as it were, in her own right, and which does not depend upon her connection with the man'.[12] On the contrary, in Gen. 1: 27, it is, as a matter of fact, only about the man that it is said expressly that he was created in the image of God: 'So God created man (*aeth-haadam*)[13] in his own image, in the image of God created he him (*otho*)'. One cannot avoid suspecting that Miss Thrall has pressed the texts in a certain direction, and in this way she succeeds in reading into them a view of woman easily reconcilable with the equality ideals of the twentieth century.

Miss Thrall, who belongs to the post-Liberal era which has rediscovered the importance of the Old Testament to theology, tries to find further support for the ordination of women to the priesthood in the prophetesses of the Old Testament, who must have had 'the same direct and unmediated contact with God as their male counterparts, and the same direct apprehension of his Word'.[14] So they form an exception to the normal position of women in Israel and Judaism, where 'women, in fact, were theologically of the same status as Gentiles'.[15] According to Miss Thrall and the authorities she refers to, the prophets of the Old Testament are types of the apostles of the New Testament.[16] And the conclusion is thus self-evident. Now Miss Thrall herself admits that 'we may explain the existence of women prophets by regarding them as types of the women members of the Church'.[17] So her proof on this point is far from conclusive. Everything depends on how 'the existence and status of women within the redeemed community'[18] is interpreted. The analogy between the prophets of the Old Testament and the apostles of the New is not to be pressed. Prophecy could never be fixed to a certain ministry. And there is certainly more in the apostolic ministry than the prophetic feature. So this instance of a view on woman, similar to the modern one, to be found in Holy Scripture, has to be rejected as untenable.

2. *The New Testament*

THE strongest apparent instance in the New Testament of a view of the relation between man and woman based on the ideal of equality, is Gal. 3: 28: 'There is neither Jew nor Greek, there is neither bond nor free, there is neither male and female: for ye are all one in Christ Jesus'. The passage invites comparison with the daily thanksgiving of the pious Jew that he has not been made a Gentile, a bondman or a woman.[19] These three classes are all excluded from full religious membership of Israel, even in Orthodox Judaism today. Women are of course not able to enter the covenant of circumcision. On the other hand a Gentile woman may take the baptism of proselytes, which women who are to be received into Judaism still have to undergo. When circumcision in the Christian Church was displaced by the sacrament of baptism, the woman became, with regard to the rite of initiation, quite equal to the man. Gal. 3: 28 is in a context concerning the precise relation between baptism and circumcision. The meaning of the passage is apparently that the woman in the New Covenant, which is based upon baptism instead of circumcision, like the Gentile and the bondman, has full membership in the people of God, with all the promises and all the obligations that this membership brings.

Now the question is: What conclusions are to be drawn from the revolution in the religious place of the woman that the New Testament undoubtedly brings, compared to her position in the Old Testament and in Judaism? Krister Stendahl[20] regards this passage as an instance of a fundamental theological view of the religious equality between man and woman, a view which has to admit consistently the equality of the woman with the man, entitling her to ordination to the priesthood, no less than to a new position in family and community. This consequence was not immediately drawn by the Church, but nor did the words 'there is neither bond nor free' at once bring the abolition of slavery, Stendahl says. He does not deny that the New Testament contains texts which militate against drawing the consequences from the full incorporation of the woman into God's people which Stendahl wants to draw. He even admits that the basic view of the relation between man and woman in the New Testament is 'plainly Jewish',[21] i.e., it regards the woman as subordinated to the man as 'the weaker vessel' (1 Pet. 3: 7). The New Testament bases this view of the woman on the Creation (Gen. 2: 18f) and the Fall (Gen. 3: 16) stories.[22] But this view, which characterises the 'Haustafel' of the New Testament (Eph. 5: 22ff, Col. 3: 18f, Tit. 2: 5f, 1 Pet. 2: 18f) 1 Cor. 11: 3f, 14: 34f, 1 Tim. 2: 11-15, is broken through, according to Stendahl, at once by Gal. 3: 28, by the admonitions to Christian men to respect their wives as 'heirs together of the grace of life'[23] and by 1 Cor. 11: 11f: 'Nevertheless neither is the man without the woman, neither the woman without the man, in the Lord. For as the woman is of the man, even so is the man also by the woman; but all things are of God.' In the last passage, the understanding based upon the Creation story of Gen. 2 predominates: 'The woman is *of* the man' (ἐκ τοῦ ἀνδρος, cf.Gen. 2: 22f), while 'the man is *by* the woman' (διὰ τῆς γυναικος). What is expressed here is a mutual dependence and completing, not equality, side by side. Nor is it possible to maintain that the fundamental view, based upon the Creation story in Gen. 2, is broken by Col. 3: 19 and Eph. 5: 25, 28. The women are admonished to be subordinate (ὑποτασσεσθαι) to their husbands, the husbands to love (ἀγαπαν) their wives. If, like Stendahl, one interpreted the admonition to men to love their wives as expressing a tendency towards equality between man and woman, one would also have to interpret Christ's love for his Church as implying the abrogation of the subordination of the Church to Christ. For the subordination of women to their husbands is parallel to the subordination of the Church to her Lord, as the love of the men for their wives is compared to the love of Christ for his Church (Eph. 5: 24f). From a modern point of view one would of course expect admonitions to mutual love between husband and wife. But as a matter of fact there are none in these texts. One would have to over-press the exhortation in 1 Thess. 4: 4f, 'that every one of you should know how to possess his vessel in sanctification and honour, not in the lust of concupiscence, even as the Gentiles which know not God', if one were to find anything there that 'breaks through the Creation-conditioned fundamental view', as Stendahl says. 1 Pet. 3: 7 must be placed along with Gal. 3: 28 as expressing the New Testament conception of the woman as a full member of the people of God, and so co-heir of its promises. However, the verse also speaks of the woman as 'the weaker vessel' and apparently presupposes the subordination of the woman to the man, which is enforced in the preceding verses. It is clear that the apostle himself has not felt any contrast between a 'Creation-conditioned fundamental view' and the conception of the woman as συνκληρονομος χαριτος ζωης. Is it possible that there is such a contrast, although the author was not conscious of it? Is there a contrast between Gal. 3: 28 and 1 Cor. 14: 34f, although St. Paul did not feel it? That is what Stendahl wants to maintain. He declares in a rather high-flown passage: 'We must ask, whether the general biblical view . . . is not disfigured and deep-frozen, if the fundamental view and the tendencies that prove to be on their way to burst this fundamental view are allowed to make a harmonious peace within the frame of the Canon'.[24] But are there really any indications at all in the New Testament texts that the authors themselves were conscious of expressing any 'tendencies'[25] towards bursting that relation between man and woman which was founded by God, when he created male and female? If not, is it then proper to say that those who do not find any such tendencies are trying to harmonise the texts? Rather one might say that they try to take the texts as they find them, while Stendahl, according to *a priori* hermeneutical principles, attempts to undo that 'harmonious peace', which undoubtedly is there to the *authors*, between the first and the second half of 1 Pet. 3: 7, and between Gal. 3: 28 and 1 Cor. 14. 34f. If Stendahl has not managed to understand how the New Testament writers have been able to avoid feeling that contrast which he himself feels, that is his problem. But the task of the interpreter cannot be to read contrasts into the text, which are alien to the author, but to try to understand exactly what the author meant, when he wrote the text. As a working hypothesis at least, one ought to presume that the author himself best understands what he has written. Stendahl has hardly been able to show that the view of Gal. 3: 28 of the relation between man and woman, that the woman has full membership in the new Israel, must bring consequences for the place of the woman in the family, in the community, as well as in regard to ordination to the priesthood, which the New Testament itself does not draw.

Finally one must ask why Stendahl wants to find the deepest 'Christian' view on man and woman precisely in Gal. 3: 28, which might be interpreted according to a modern conception of the relation between man and woman. If there were a contrast between Gal. 3: 28 and the Pauline passages expressing the subordination of women, why could not Stendahl equally maintain that Gal. 3: 28 expresses 'dangerous' tendencies towards the dissolution of the general biblical view on the relation between man and woman? In other words: What is Stendahl's selective principle, the selective principle that compels him to make the view he finds in Gal. 3: 28 the authoritative view, compared to the view he finds in passages like 1 Cor. 14: 34f? One cannot avoid the suspicion that in the end the fact that Gal. 3: 28 might be interpreted as expressing something like modern opinions about the equality between men and women is this selective principle. So Stendahl has himself fallen a victim to that method of 'Liberal theology' which he describes in a way which is very much to the point:

> Thus one can rightly maintain that the exegesis of Liberal theology often proved incapable of descriptive and objective historical research, and it is evident that the reason for this was that its hermeneutic, its principles of interpretation, were allowed to adjust the material so that the texts were not given any opportunity to speak their original language. The application for our own time was built into the exegesis. Everything becomes arranged to suit apologetics. The distance between the centuries is overcome too easily and too swiftly. Whether one accepts these hermeneutic principles or not, it is evident that they colour the description and lead to an anachronistic sifting of the material.

Again, on St. Paul's mention of women as fellow-workers (Rom. 16: 2, 3, Phil. 4: 3)[26] the question is applicable: Why are *these* texts supposed to express the real view of St. Paul on woman? It cannot be a correct method of interpreting texts to range one group of texts in the material against another, if you are going to interpret the whole material. The right procedure must be to try to understand how St. Paul was able to count women among his fellow-workers, although he did not allow them to teach (διδασκειν) or to speak in the Church (λαλειν εν τη εκκλησια) according to 1 Tim. 2: 12 and 1 Cor. 14: 34. If the term 'fellow-worker', even 'in the Gospel', could imply any sort of priestly position, then all lay Christians would be excluded from being fellow-workers in the Gospel with the ordained ministers. Such a clericalism would be alien both to the New Testament and to the primitive Church. The whole people of God has the mission 'to proclaim the triumphs of him who has called you out of darkness into his marvellous light' (1 Pet. 2: 9). But everybody is not, for that reason, an apostle, prophet or teacher (1 Cor. 12: 29). The fact that 'women . . . are called to share in the apostolic task of the New Israel'[27] does not imply their vocation to the apostolic ministry *within* the Church, the mission to be a pastor to God's flock (Jn. 21: 15f, Acts 20: 28, 1 Pet. 5: 2f). Only when the apostolate of all Christians to the world, 'the priesthood of all believers', has been forgotten, do people get the impression that, in order to participate in the Church's preaching of the Gospel to the world, the woman has to participate in what, according to Lutheran terminology, is called 'the special priesthood', the ministry of ἐπίσκοπος aud ποιμήν in the Church, the special tasks of which do not primarily concern the proclamation of the Gospel to the world (the task of all baptised Christians) but the feeding of the flock (Jn. 21: 15f), the steward's administration of the household (Lk. 12: 41f). When the tasks which should belong to all Christians have been reserved for priests and bishops, those special tasks which should belong to the pastoral ministry are liable to disappear, as in some places to a great extent they have done.

So, having confused 'special' and 'universal' priesthood, people think that (1) when the New Testament speaks of women who, had positions in the Church, this must imply their having been 'clergy' in one way or another and (2) women lack opportunities in the present-day Church, if they do not become priests. Characteristic of Liberal conceptions is the principle of equality between the sexes and the demand, based on this principle of equality, for equal rights in regard to all posts in the community. Characteristic of New Testament conceptions is the doctrine of the Church as the Body of Christ with members of different kinds.[28] 'For by one Spirit are we all baptised into one body, whether we be Jews or Gentiles, whether we be bond or free'—and one might add: 'whether we be male or female'—says St. Paul in 1 Cor. 12: 13; but a few verses later he asks: 'Are we all apostles? are we all prophets? are we all teachers?'

The relation between 1 Cor. 11: 5, which suggests that the woman can pray and prophesy in public, and 1 Cor. 14: 34, with its absolute prohibition of any speaking by a woman in the Church, is a problem. The hypothesis that the later passage is an interpolation has been proposed. Miss Thrall convincingly refutes this theory in her book.[29] However this may be, the prohibition against speaking is found in at least one other passage in the New Testament, 1 Tim. 2: 11f.[30] Nor is 1 Cor. 11: 5 itself any support to the principle of equality. Here St. Paul demands that the woman, as distinct from the man, cover her head because she 'is the glory of the man', while 'he is the image and glory of God' (v.7). Although uncertainty as to the extent of the prohibition may exist, the constant principle of the woman's subordination to the man is clear and evident.[31]

One is tempted to speak about a desperate need for arguments, when some authors[32] refer to the uncertainty among the older exegetes whether Rom. 16: 7 mentions a man called Junias or a woman called

Junia, who, according to an interpretation which is possible although not very probable, was counted among the apostles. Although, philologically, there is a possibility that these exegetes were right, it seems rather improbable, in view of what St. Paul in other places has said about women, that Rom. 16: 7 mentions any apostle Junia. This obscure passage has to be interpreted in the light of the clear ones; that seems to be a sound principle for the interpretation of texts.

A theory original to Miss Thrall, as far as I know, is that the Blessed Virgin in the moment of the Annunciation fulfils a priestly function, being then the representative of the people of Israel before God. For this is 'the traditional function of the male priesthood of Israel. . . . So that, if we say that the function of Mary is of significance in determining the function of women in the Church, the conclusion we must draw is that it is possible for a woman to assume the priestly function of representing the people before God'.[33] So the syllogism is:

(a) Only priests can represent Israel before God.
(b) Mary represents Israel before God.
(c) Consequently Mary is a priest.

Now one has to question whether the priests and Mary represented Israel before God in the same way. The priests represented the people before God in the cult, above all at the sacrifices. The direction of this representation goes upward: from the people through the priests to God. The Blessed Virgin represents the people before God as receiving the Word of God in faith. The direction points downward: from God through Mary to the people. To receive the Word of God is a typically *lay* function, which every member of the people of Israel, both in the old and in the new Covenant, may and ought to fulfil.

3. *Jesus of Nazareth*

CHARACTERISTIC of the Protestant theology of the turn of the century was the contrast found between 'the historic Jesus' and 'the second founder of Christianity', Paul. It is well known that this is a permanent source for polemics in modern theology. However, when people look for support in Jesus of Nazareth against Paul's prohibition of women speaking and his teaching on subordination, it is nowadays mainly in popular circles which have not kept up with the development of theology since the turn of the century. Although one must feel sceptical from the beginning of all attempts to set 'the historic Jesus' against Paul, we must ask: Is there any reason to suppose that Jesus of Nazareth had a view of woman like the Liberal one?

The first difficulty in answering this question is how to reach the view of Jesus himself, independent of Paul, John and *Gemeindetheologie*.[34] Our sources for the teaching of Jesus consist almost solely in the four canonical Gospels, and these are written by people who represent *Gemeindetheologie*. Is there any criterion by which it would be possible to separate that which originates from Jesus of Nazareth himself, from that which is *Gemeindetheologie*, Paul and John? Such a criterion ought to be sought from a reliable source outside those circles which are determined by *Gemeindetheologie*, Paul and John. But such a source does not exist. We are restricted to purely internal evidence, if we want to separate the genuinely dominical material in the Gospels, from that which is Pauline, Johannine, etc. Such internal evidence we might have had, if we thought we knew the theology of Paul, John, Peter etc. so well that we were able to state when a saying by Jesus, handed on by the evangelists, could not be reconciled with their theology. Then there might be reasons to suppose that this saying was so undoubtedly authentic dominical material that the evangelists dared not suppress it, or re-edit it, according to their own purposes. Is there such a saying or action by Jesus which might justify the supposition that his view of woman was more like the modern one than St. Paul's was? I have not found any saying of Jesus to support such a notion. The behaviour of Jesus towards women shows a more free view than was usual in his day. Most important is the story of Jesus and the Samaritan woman in John 4. It has been employed, e.g., by Dr. Margit Sahlin in her book quoted above.[35] In John 4: 27 it is said that his disciples 'marvelled that he talked with a woman'.[36] Dr. Sahlin comments thus on the passage: 'As so often they met in Jesus the "otherwise", the secret that was still hidden—"What I am doing now, ye do not now understand, but in the future. . . .".' This action, like the Lord's commission to Mary (John 20: 17) or the other women (Mt. 28: 10, Mk. 16: 7) to proclaim his resurrection to the disciples, the fact that Martha and Mary may be counted among the closest friends of Jesus (Lk. 10: 38ff, John 11: 12), that women remained standing to the last at the cross of Jesus (Mk. 15: 40f, John 19: 25), that Jesus points to women as examples of faith (Mt. 15: 28, 26: 13, Mk. 12: 41f, Lk. 10- 42 etc.), and in his parables describes female figures as willingly as male ones,[37] are 'signs', 'parable actions', which demonstrate the new way of life in God's Kingdom. 'The new age' is breaking in: 'it is there already, but visible only in glimpses and hints, which faith alone recognises. Also the closest disciples of Jesus were too much dependent on the inherited views of their own generation to be able quite to grasp this revolutionising new view, which Jesus gives, not in theoretical expositions, or reform programmes, but in actions which point forward.'[38] Faced with this sort of argument, it is necessary to ask what new factor has been added to enable Dr. Sahlin to understand these 'parable actions' better than the disciples of Jesus who told us about them, better than most interpreters of the texts up to modern times? It is hard to deny that the new factor is the Liberal view of woman. If one knows of the conception of woman's social equality with man beforehand, one may of course say that certain actions of Jesus are closer to the Liberal view than is the Jewish view, which has been predominant up until our own day. So these actions of Jesus might be interpreted as 'signs' for 'the new age'. But one must ask: Which 'new age'? The 'new age' of the New Testament, an eschatological idea, or the 'new age' of Liberalism, our own age? If one interprets the texts in a purely historical and philological manner, the only thing which can be stated is that Jesus behaved more freely towards women than traditional Judaism did and does.[39] However, even Professor Stendahl turns away from the idea that this had any theological importance: 'It will be difficult to find any elements in the Gospels which break through this fundamental view of Palestinian Judaism. Those sayings of Jesus which touch the relation between man and woman all fall within this view. The contrast between Talmudic school sayings and the more non-professional and popular character of the activity of Jesus explains more than sufficiently the prominent role women play in his activity and the place of domestic duties in his parable sayings. The schoolroom or the judgment-seat of the rabbi is the milieu of Talmudic wisdom, but the wandering preaching of Jesus brought him closer to the life of the people.'[40] Incidentally, if the actions of Jesus towards women are to be regarded as 'signs' for the attitude a much later Church should adopt to the ordination of women to the priesthood, why could not his choice of men only to be apostles be equally regarded as a 'sign'? If Jesus in other cases suggested by 'signs' the 'revolutionising new view' of the relation between the sexes, why did he not above all do so at such a central point as at the institution of the Eucharist? The theory of accommodation may be an excellent way of explaining why Jesus acted in a manner in which one might wish that he had not acted, but it will always give a strong impression of wishful thinking.[41] As when the Rationalism of the eighteenth century launched the theory, the feeling cannot be avoided that it is rather a question of accommodating Jesus to the opinions of our own age, than of Jesus having accommodated himself to those of his.

The result of this investigation is evident. Those who have wanted to find the Liberal view of woman as in all respects equal to man, in the Bible, in the New Testament, or in the life and teaching of Jesus of Nazareth, have worked according to methods elsewhere abandoned by scientific exegesis. Only by these methods, and according to a selective principle, settled in advance but seldom plainly expressed, have they been able to unearth some ideas, in certain strata of the material, which agree with the modern view of woman. Only on this basis have they recommended the ordination of women to the priesthood as possible, or even desirable, from a biblical point of view. In other words, it is an illusion that the Bible, the New Testament or Jesus of Nazareth teaches a view of woman which is in harmony with the principle of the equal rights of the sexes in all fields, in the family, in the community and in the Church. This does not, of course, necessarily mean that Liberal thinking about woman is untenable in itself. Liberal ideas about the total equality between man and woman in all fields are wrong only if one sets out from the belief that the biblical view must be the right view. But it is impossible to establish any harmony between that view of woman which is the view of the Bible, and that which is the view of Liberalism, without changing one of them on essential points. Those who hold a Liberal view of woman are not asked to abjure that opinion. But, in the name of intellectual honesty, they are asked to acknowledge that their view of woman is the one of Liberalism, not the one of the Bible, the New Testament, or the historic Jesus.

NOTES

[1] Art. 3. Cf. also the Universal Declaration of Human Rights, adopted by the General Assembly of the United Nations on the tenth day of December 1948, art. 1, 16, 23.
[2] Except perhaps in Bultmann's school of *Entmythologisierung*, which however regards Jesus himself as bound to mythical conceptions.
[3] eg as they are described by Professor Krister Stendahl in the most outstanding Swedish book supporting the ordination of women to the priesthood, *Kvinnan Samhället Kyrkan* (1958), p. 140f.
[4] pp. 28f, 73.
[5] p. 28.
[6] p. 36.
[7] p. 73.
[8] p. 36, 74.
[9] p. 73.
[10] p. 29.
[11] p. 36.
[12] p. 32.
[13] Miss Thrall, for some reason which she does not tell the reader, states that both Adam and Eve 'really are the *adam* of Genesis 1' (p. 35). But why then the change from *otho* to *otham* in the latter half of the verse?
[14] p. 50.
[15] p. 45. But this is not quite correct. A Jew is only allowed to marry Jewish women. Cf. Ezra 9: 10.
[16] p. 50, 64, 93f, 98.
[17] p. 51.
[18] Cf. H. Riesenfeld, *The Ministry in the New Testament* (*The Root of the Vine*, ed. A. Fridrichsen, 1953).
[19] In *Shacharith*: barukh atha adonai aeloheinu maelaekh ha'olam shaelo 'asanni goj . . . shaelo 'assanni 'aebhedh . . . shaeló 'asanni ijsha. The striking parallel has been pointed out to me by Dr. Hans Kosmala, Director of the Swedish Theological Institute in Jerusalem.
[20] Op.cit. p. 159f.
[21] p. 152.
[22] p. 156.
[23] 1 Pet. 3: 7. Cf. Col. 3: 19. Eph. 5: 25, 28.
[24] p. 161f.
[25] Stendahl is rather cautious in his mode of expression.
[26] In the Swedish debate, among others, Margit Sahlin, *Ordets tjänst i en förändrad varld*.
[27] Thrall, op.cit. p. 90.
[28] In the Swedish debate this contrast was emphasised especially by Bishop A. Nygren at the Church Assembly in 1957.
[29] Op.cit. p. 77ff.
[30] Maybe, too, in Rev. 2: 20—it is thus interpreted eg by B. Gärtner in *Kvinnan och ämbetet enligt Skriften och beknänelsen* (1958), s. 86f.

³¹ Attempts to solve this problem have been made, in Sweden (among others) by Hugo Odeberg in his Commentary on the Letters to the Corinthians (1944), p. 263, where he maintains that 1 Cor. 11 speaks about an inner meeting by the Christians in more free forms than the public service with which 1 Cor. 14 is concerned; and by B. Reicke in *Kvinnan och ämbetet enligt Skriften och bekännelsen* (1958), p. 29, who thinks that 'the prophecy' of 1 Cor. 11: 5 is a 'free witness', while 'the speaking' of 1 Cor. 14: 34 is 'a sermon', built upon the Word of God delivered through the apostles.

³² Margit Sahlin (1959), p. 38, Harald Sahlin in *Svensk Kyrkotidning*, 1959, pp. 655, 739. Cf. answer to H. Sahlin by L. Hartman, *Svensk Kyrkotidning*, 1959, pp. 692, 754.

³³ p. 87.

³⁴ I refrain from discussing the relation between these. I only want to use the terms which were generally employed by the Protestant theologians from the turn of the century.

³⁵ p. 16f.

³⁶ Γυναικος stands in the indefinite form. The translation 'the woman' (AV) is hardly correct.

³⁷ p. 15, 17.

³⁸ p. 16.

³⁹ On the other hand it is hardly possible to maintain that these actions by Jesus go any farther than Gal. 3: 28. If they are 'signs' of anything at all, they are rather 'signs' of the full membership of women in the people of God, which Gal. 3: 28 speaks about.

⁴⁰ *Op. cit.* p. 153.

⁴¹ This is conspicuous in Dr. Sahlin's book, p. 34f, eg when it is said, 'that the watch-nights of the disciples in desert places or in Gethsemane were hardly suited to respectable women' and 'to take women about with one on the roads out to the life of the wilderness would hardly have been becoming for the one who had an urgent message to bring' etc.

Women and the Priesthood of the Church

E. L. MASCALL

From the earliest days of the Christian Church down to almost the present time the incapacity of women to be admitted to the historic Holy Orders of the Catholic Church has been not so much argued as taken for granted. This is presumably the reason for the brief and, it must be admitted, inadequate consideration of the question which is found in the Supplement to the *Summa Theologica*[1]; the author has clearly more pressing and controversial matters which demand his attention. That the deaconesses who finally became extinct round about the eleventh century did not constitute a "Holy" or major Order was convincingly shown by the late Dr. N. P. Williams in a speech which he made in the Convocation of Canterbury in June 1938 and which is reprinted at the end of Dean Kemp's memoir[2]; as he remarked, the *diaconissate* cannot even be shown to have existed as an "order" of any sort before the fourth century. In recent years, however, the question has been raised more than once, and the claim has been made that the unbroken practice of the Church in refraining from conferring Holy Orders upon women rests upon no theological basis but merely upon social convention or sheer male self-assertiveness; and it is sometimes suggested, in spite of the absence of evidence, that throughout the Christian centuries there have been thousands of Christian women who were thirsting to exercise the priesthood but were sternly and unfeelingly frustrated by the domineering male authorities. Discussion has been made the more difficult by the fact that the various Christian bodies and their theologians differ widely among themselves as to what the nature and functions of the Christian ministry are; it is roughly true that, if a Catholic is asked "Do you think that women ought to be ordained?" he will immediately think of a woman standing at the altar celebrating the Eucharist, while a

---

[1] *Supp.* xxxix. 1.   [2] E. W. Kemp, *N. P. Williams*, pp. 185f.

Protestant, if asked the same question, will think of a woman standing in the pulpit preaching a sermon. It must therefore be made plain from the start that the question with which we are concerned is whether women are capable of admission to the "Holy" or major orders of the Catholic Church, and in particular to the priesthood and episcopate, whether they are capable of receiving that indelible "character" of Holy Orders to which Archbishops Frederick Temple and Maclagan more than once referred in their reply to Pope Leo XIII[1].

It is of the greatest importance that a matter such as this, in which emotional and irrational reactions are only too easily aroused on either side, should be discussed upon a strictly theological plane. This must not, however, be taken to mean that it is to be conducted upon purely deductive lines, and that the conclusions, in order to be valid, must be shown to follow with apodictic logical cogency by a series of syllogistic steps from certain basic and undeniable premises of the Christian religion. Only the most arid kinds of scholastic theology have been content to take that course, and even then one is often tempted to suspect that the syllogistic form of the argument is in fact an artificial and *ex post facto* construction; certainly Anglican theology has never adopted that as its ideal. The threefold appeal to Scripture, tradition and reason which is characteristic of Anglican theology is far richer and deeper in its scope. Theological investigation of the legitimacy of any actual or proposed course of action will be concerned far more with its general coherence with the whole body of Christian life and thought than with *a priori* deductions. Thus, for example, it would be extremely difficult to prove beyond all manner of doubt on purely *a priori* grounds that the children of Christian parents ought normally to be baptised in infancy, but it is perfectly easy to show that the practice is thoroughly consistent with the nature of the Body of Christ and of sacramental grace as Catholic tradition understands them. So, with our present question, what we want to know is whether the unbroken tradition of the Church for the first nineteen centuries of its existence in restricting Holy Orders to persons of the male sex, can be seen to be organically articulated with the whole *corpus* of Catholic theology or whether it has no such connection and is therefore to be looked on as nothing more than a rather strange accident of history. Such an enquiry can rightly claim to be theological in the true sense of the word.

[1] *Responsio* . . . , XV, XVIII, XIX.

Non-theological considerations

This does not mean that there may not be arguments of very great weight which are not theological but rather practical in their bearing. Thus, for example, the fact that admission of women to Holy Orders would put an additional and extremely serious obstacle in the way of future reunion with the Roman Catholic and Orthodox Churches and would destroy our already achieved unity with the Old Catholic Churches should be a quite sufficient deterrent to anyone who does not identify Christianity to all intents and purposes with Protestantism. Furthermore, the virtue of Christian humility itself would seem to demand from the Christian theologian the admission that an unbroken and universal practice of Catholic Christendom is almost certain to have some profound theological basis, even if he himself has not yet discovered what it is. Indeed, the main method by which Christian theology advances is by trying to penetrate more fully than before into the theological meaning of the Church's life and practice, rather than by discarding as trivial those elements of them which it has not so far thought out. Only so is theology kept in vital touch with the life of the Body of Christ and saved from becoming the most abstract of all academic pursuits. Thus N. P. Williams, in the paper to which I have already referred, having put the question "Is it possible for persons of the female sex to become members of the historic ministry instituted by Christ (as distinct from other ministries instituted by the Church, or by 'man's authority' alone)?", points out that, "until a few years ago, it would have been universally assumed throughout Christendom, that the example of our Lord in choosing only men to be his Apostles (not conferring any sort of ministerial authority or jurisdiction even upon his blessed Mother), the emphatic language used by St Paul in condemning female ministrations, the universal custom of the Church of Christ, constituted an overwhelming weight of authority against any such idea." Referring to the modern suggestions that this limitation was due only to the contingent conditions of time and place and that the Church's custom is nothing but "a manifestation of unreasoning conservatism", he went on to say:

The assumption that our Lord was so much a slave of contemporary ideas that he "could not" have broken through them, is not calculated to encourage great confidence in him, merely considered as a human Teacher; the *onus probandi* lies with those who make it, not on those who, trusting him as the incarnate Truth, desire in this matter to do what he did and nothing else. So also with the implied repudiation of the authority of the New Testament and of the Church; for Churchmen at any rate, the *onus probandi* must be deemed to rest upon those who would defy these august authorities, not on those who would maintain them.

Williams was at pains to observe that his contention amounted

> ... not so much to the thesis that it is dogmatically certain that women cannot receive "Holy Orders", but ... to the thesis that there is an overwhelming probability, based upon the example of our Lord, the teaching of the New Testament, and the universal practice of the Church, that they cannot, and that no serious reason has been adduced for supposing that they can,

and he summed up this part of his argument by saying:

> Those who venerate the example of Christ, the commands of St Paul, and the practice of the Church, will feel that no power short of an Oecumenical Council—perhaps only an Oecumenical Council enlightened by a special revelation of the will of God—could dare to assume the responsibility of modifying or altering what comes to us upon authority so mysterious and august.[1]

For Williams clearly this argument was conclusive, but he was well aware that arguments from pure authority have little force with twentieth-century Englishmen; nor would he himself have tolerated the notion that Christ, the Bible and the Church would combine in imposing upon Christians so drastic a discipline as the disqualification of half the Church's members from the reception of Holy Orders unless there was some reason for this. And he went on in fact to build up a very imposing argument to which it is difficult to do justice without quoting it in full in his own sonorous prose. It is based upon the "well-known, though mysterious, affinity between religious emotion and sex-emotion", in virtue of

[1] op. cit., p. 193-5

which "the stimulation of the religious instinct may, by a kind of subconscious reverberation, under certain circumstances, simultaneously stimulate that *per se* less supernatural instinct which is so closely allied to it". He insists, therefore, on "the utmost importance, indeed . . . the most stringent necessity, that the personality of the officiant in any form of divine worship, as of any others who in any degree participate in the leadership in worship . . . should not be such as to convey, even accidentally, the very slightest avoidable suggestion, of the kind which we have indicated, to the imaginations of any present". "The natural conclusion," he maintains, "is that only those ought to be admitted to Holy Orders whose personalities are not likely in a liturgical or sacramental atmosphere to exercise any distracting effect upon worshippers of the opposite sex to their own," and he claims that

> men as such are much less likely to be an involuntary cause of distraction to women, under the circumstances of public worship, than women are to men; that this is a permanent fact of human nature, which can no more be abolished by modern progress than the law of gravitation can be abolished by modern progress,

while he hastens to add:

> Although this fact may seem to result in a privilege for men, it does not imply any moral superiority on their part over women, but, if anything, the opposite; it is based, paradoxically enough, upon their greater weakness (in this regard) and susceptibility.[1]

This argument of Williams's may have a good deal of force in it, but it must be noticed that it is an argument of expediency based upon considerations of psychology and is not in the strict sense theological. It would, as he remarks, exclude women from *any* visible official participation in worship, as choristers or acolytes for example; and, unless the senses of sight and hearing are (as perhaps they are) to be considered as altogether different from each other in the relevant respect, it would appear to exclude them from almost any participation in an invisible choir also; this last restriction would go beyond the limitations imposed even by the Roman or Eastern Orthodox Churches. At its best, Williams's argu-

[1] ibid., p. 195-8

ment is mainly an argument from expediency—an argument that women *ought not* to be given a prominent part in public worship, rather than an argument that they *cannot* receive Holy Orders and, unless it is reinforced by more strictly theological considerations, I think many people will, not altogether unreasonably, feel that the very real dangers to which he points might be kept within bounds by suitable safeguards if, on other grounds, the ordination of women was desirable. In any case, I think a good many people will feel that it is an argument stated rather too much from the male standpoint, and from the standpoint of a very normal male at that. Without exaggerating the dangers involved or underrating the power of grace to neutralise them, it would be unrealistic to ignore the sexual element in the impression which the personality of a male officiant may have upon either females or homosexually inclined males in his congregation, and it is not overwhelmingly obvious that this effect is necessarily weaker than that which a female officiant would be likely to have upon a normal male. Furthermore, Williams's argument becomes a little incoherent at the end. He rightly makes it plain that his contentions apply only to the strictly *religious* context. "Where the atmosphere is entirely secular, or unemotional, none of the foregoing considerations have the slightest application. There is no reason whatever why a woman should not deliver a university lecture before a mixed audience, preside at a meeting of a board of directors, sit on the Bench as a magistrate, deliver a speech in the House of Commons, act as a cabinet minister or even as the sovereign." And he insists that there is a "diversity of functions which the difference of the sexes involves, and always (so long as human nature is constituted as it is) must involve. Probably," he adds, "few of those who have been the most zealous champions of the equality of the sexes would wish to see women holding commissions in the fighting services, or deprived of their customary right to be yielded seats in trains and omnibuses by gentlemen."[1] However, to a generation which *has* seen women holding commissions in the fighting services (and to a future generation in which the customary right of women to seats in public vehicles may have vanished altogether) this illustration may seem a little dated, and one may wonder whether, if he had lived in 1850, Williams would not have been as horrified at the idea of a woman being a don or a chairman of directors as being an

[1] ibid., p. 199.

officer in the A.T.S. Furthermore, even in public worship the Church has not been quite as restrictive as Williams's argument would seem to suggest. In the Orthodox Church a woman can frequently be seen performing very prominent functions as a reader, the bride at a wedding is (according to the Western view) the minister of a public sacrament; the godmother at a baptism, the superior at a profession, while they cannot be described as *leading* public worship, are taking a very prominent and essential part in it; and the part that a female sovereign plays at her coronation is still fresh in the minds of English people. While Williams may very well be right in emphasising the wisdom with which the Church has severely limited the part played by women in the ministerial functions of public worship, it cannot be argued that that limitation is absolute, and it hardly seems possible to build upon psychological considerations an argument for the incapacity of women to receive Holy Orders. If such an argument were to be made cogent it might be necessary to enquire whether, from this psychological standpoint, the celebration of the Eucharist was in a radically different category from the conducting of other services and the preaching of sermons; but, however suggestive arguments derived from psychology may be, I cannot avoid the conviction that the fundamental considerations must be not psychological but theological.

A theological approach

Those who advocate the ordination of women usually start from the undeniable fact that, whereas in Judaism women occupied an essentially inferior position, if for no other reason than that they were physically unable to be admitted into the Covenant by the rite of circumcision[1], in Christianity the water of baptism and the unction of the Spirit are available indifferently to men and women alike. "As many of you as were baptised into Christ did put on Christ. There can be neither Jew nor Greek, there can be neither bond nor free, there can be no male and female; for ye all are one man in Christ Jesus."[2] The bearing of the argument is, how-

[1] ch. M. E. Thrall, *The Ordination of Women to the Priesthood*, p. 44f. for an examination of the Old Testament evidence.
[2] Gal. iii. 27-8.

ever all the other way. For it is this same primitive Church, which is appealed to as witnessing to the absolute equality of all Christians, both male and female, in their status as members of the Body of Christ through baptism, which restricted the Church's ministerial functions to men. And behind the action of the Church in this matter there lies the example of her Founder, who (as we see for example in his condemnation of the Jewish attitude to divorce) was full of sympathy for women but who nevertheless founded the Church's ministry by giving it a purely male Apostolate. It would be absurd to suppose that in doing this Christ was depriving women of their legitimate rights, and misleading his Church as to their true status, as a concession to the conventions and prejudices of the time; even his enemies never accused him of conventionality or cowardice, and it would ill become his disciples in the twentieth century to do so. When we find our Lord and the primitive Church restricting the ministry to males *in spite of the emphasis laid by both alike upon the absolute equality of women with men as members of the New Israel which is the Body of Christ,* is it not natural to assume that there must be some very deep and significant reason in the nature of things for this restriction?

Mrs. F. Cruttwell Blomfield has made this point very tellingly in her little book *Wonderful Order* in the following words:

> Not only is the Sacred Ministry something possessing its own sacramental method of generation; it is also, from the first, composed of men. Our Lord cannot be supposed insensitive to the gifts and powers of women; he had many of them amongst his disciples. The Church has relied on the ministerial order as Christ designed it: the order he instituted when he chose a band of men to be his apostles. Holy Order is not something invented by man, but is created (or invented) by Christ himself. He did not ordain any of the women disciples, though they were surely just as capable of making good clergy as any of those who now aspire to the priesthood.
>
> It may be said that this was because the Jewish Church knew nothing of priestesses; and that it would have been therefore too revolutionary an action to begin to make them in the early Church. But the absence of priestesses in Israel has itself to be explained, before this can be used as an argument for changing the plan. Was Israel wrong? It is absurd to suppose (as some do) that the idea of the "priest-

hood of women" emerges as a sign of progress and evolution in our own day. It is of immemorial antiquity; it is found in the very dawn of history. The ancient world and all its great civilisations had religions with goddesses as well as gods, and priestesses as well as priests. But Israel knew them not. There, we find an occasional prophetess; but only men were priests. Our Lord was never afraid to break with the religion of Israel when he deemed it right to do so—as he did in the matter of the Sabbath. The change of the weekly holy-day seemed then shockingly revolutionary. Yet for all his independence our Lord confirmed the Old Testament rule of a priesthood of men. There is not the least suspicion possible that this was because he regarded women as inferior; for it is his influence which has raised them. If, then, he deliberately concentrated upon the training of twelve men to be the ministers of his Catholic Church, it would be, to say the least, the height of presumption to alter his design.[1]

Of equal relevance are the following comments made by Miss Thrall on Canon R. W. Howard's assertion that the male priesthood of Judaism was due to a one-sided reaction, in a patriarchal society, from an equally one-sided institution of a female priesthood in an earlier matriarchal period when the deity was conceived as a fertility goddess:

This argument is ingenious, but it is open to criticism. In the first place, what have these nature deities, the fertility goddesses of whom Canon Howard speaks, to do with the God of Abraham, Isaac and Jacob, the Creator of heaven and earth? To conceive of these deities as female and to worship them only by means of a female priesthood may be taking a one-sided view, but it is hardly a one-sided view of God. It is not a view of God at all, but the result of the human tendency to idolatry. And what Canon Howard is pleased to term the reaction, that is, the Biblical worship of the Lord Jehovah by means of a male priesthood, is not merely reaction or the swing of the pendulum in the opposite direction, but the recall of man from the worship of idols to the worship of the living God, and the beginning of redemptive history. The extra-biblical existence of female priesthoods appears more as a warning than as an inducement towards ordaining women, and the male priesthood of Israel is not to be viewed theologically as an example of

[1] op. cit., p. 26-7.

"Jewish inhibitions" which must be outgrown.[1]

The point as issue was lucidly stated by a writer in the *Graham Street Quarterly* of Autumn 1956, in which stress was laid on the fact that women are able in principle to perform in church all the functions which laymen as such can perform.

The true "liturgy" of the layman is to "offer" the oblations at Mass and to assist at the consummation of the sacrifice by communicating. Women share these privileges on completely equal terms with men. They are admitted to the sacraments—baptism, confirmation, penance, marriage, unction in exactly the same way that men are. They can be churchwardens, "sidesmen", parish councillors, and members of the Church Assembly. We take all this for granted, but Christianity is the only world-religion which treats women as God's children in exactly the same sense that men are. There is no sex-bar in the Christian Church. St Paul taught that in Jesus Christ, in his Body, there is no distinction between male and female. They are equally members of the family of the one Heavenly Father.

In consequence women can, and do, perform all the duties in church which laymen are allowed to do. For example, all the breviary offices, from the earliest times, have been recited by nuns in their chapels without any intervention or help from any priest. They worship in exactly the same way as congregations of monks do. Those communities of women who recite Morning and Evening Prayer do so among themselves with no more restrictions than are imposed on laymen. Superiors of women's communities and sisters whom they appoint, give addresses in their chapels. Deaconesses and other laywomen are licensed by bishops to do the same in parish churches. There is no objection at all to these ministrations for congregations of women and children, although some may doubt the wisdom of allowing women to officiate for mixed congregations.[2]

We may note in passing that this writer, while recognising in the last sentence by implication the force of Williams's argument, keeps it quite distinct from the question of Holy Orders. As he says, "there is no difficulty at all until we come to proposals that Holy Orders should be conferred upon

---

[1] *The Ordination of Women to the Priesthood*, p. 15. Cf. Dr. E. O. James's comments in the appendix to this pamphlet.

[2] loc. cit., p. 7.

women." And he has an extremely illuminating observation to make upon the fact that the Protestant bodies feel no difficulties about ordaining women. It is, he says, because

> the functions of their ministers are to all intents and purposes those of laymen, and we have seen that laywomen can do in church all that laymen can do. Protestant ministers instruct their congregations, conduct services, prayer meetings and bible classes. They baptise, marry and bury. In the Catholic Church all these functions, under the direction of the bishop, can be performed by any layman.[1]

In case this statement is felt to be unjust to the doctrine of the ministry held by Protestants it may be well to reinforce it from an unimpeachably Protestant source, from no less an authority than Dr Paul Tillich, who has written as follows:

> Protestantism demands a radical laicism. There are in Protestantism only laymen; the minister is a layman with a special function within the congregation; and, in addition to possessing certain personal qualities, he is qualified for the fulfilment of this function by a carefully regulated professional training. He is a non-layman solely by virtue of this training.[2]

It is important to emphasise that this agreement of Protestants upon the essential identity of the clerical and the lay status is not affected by their wide disagreement as to the way in which a man can be authorised to exercise it. Three main views seem to be held about this; one is that the authorisation comes straight from God and that all that the Church has to do (if anything) is to recognise it, one is that the authorisation comes from those who have already received it, and the third is that it comes from the local congregation as a whole. But in each case the fact remains that the functions involved, even when they include the celebration of the Eucharist, are looked upon as, in their essence, functions that any layman can exercise; it might be considered to be *improper* for him, except under very exceptional conditions, to celebrate the Eucharist, but it would not be considered to be *impossible*. Apart from his training, all that the minister has which a layman has not is *authorisation*, whether this last is conferred directly by God, by the existing ministers or by the congregation. There is no trace of the notion of *character*, as distinct from *authority*, upon which the Anglican Archbishops laid

[1] ibid., p. 10.   [2] *The Protestant Era*, ch. xi.

such stress in their reply to Leo XIII.[1] We can thus wholeheartedly agree with our Protestant brethren that, as members of Christ incorporated into his Body by baptism, there is no difference whatever in the status of a layman and that of a laywoman, and that *in principle* (for the question of what is *expedient* in any given circumstances is a different, though not an unimportant, matter) there is no difference in the functions which they can exercise or that, at most, if there is any difference it is based not upon strictly theological considerations but upon psychological and sociological considerations such as those expounded by Dr. Williams. The two essential questtions are, first, whether a priest has any essentially different status in the Body of Christ from that possessed by a lay man or woman, and, secondly,.whether, if he has, it is one which is inherently restricted to members of the male sex. If we answer both these questions in the affirmative, as the whole trend of the Church's tradition would appear to authorise us to do, it is not with any intention of disparaging either the lay person in comparison with the priest or the female in comparison with the male. Two points need to be kept in mind. The first is that, although in the Christian Church considered as an organisation there is bound to be, as in any other human association, a certain subordination of one member to another, this involves no suggestion whatever of moral or social inferiority; its nature is well described in St Paul's famous passage about the body and its members,[2] though no analogy can be perfectly adequate. Secondly, although this differentiation has certain repercussions in the organisational aspect of the Church, it is primarily not organisational but sacramental; the priest or bishop is not in the first place a ruler but a liturgical celebrant, and, although it would no doubt be inconvenient, it would not be altogether inconsistent with the Church's nature if its government was entirely exercised by the laity. To return to our point, the Catholic doctrine of the Church gives to the laity not a diminished but a vastly enhanced status, for it holds the character of the Christian lay man or woman to consist not in an external imputation of the merits of Christ, nor in a moral choice made by the

---

[1] Referring to two clauses in the Anglican ordination of a priest, they wrote: "The former, 'Receive the Holy Ghost', with what follows, together with laying on of hands, confers the general faculties and powers of priesthood (*sacerdotii*), and as is generally said, imprints the character (*characterem imprimit*). The second, together with the delivery of the Bible, gives a man the right (*auctoritatem*) to offer public service to God and to exercise authority (*potestatem exerceat*) over the Christian people who are to be entrusted to his charge in his own parish or cure" (*Resp.* XV).   [2] I Cor. xii. 12f.

individual—though both those may be and should be involved —but in his or her actual incorporation into the human nature which the Son of God united to himself in the womb of the Blessed Virgin Mary. Thus, in no merely figurative sense, the baptised Christian shares in the priesthood of Christ and he shares in it through his membership of Christ's body. Hence, to speak strictly, it is not the individual Christian but rather the Church, as Christ's body and bride made one flesh with him, which enjoys the priestly character. "The priesthood of the laity" is a somewhat misleading phrase, even when it is not used, as it so often is, not so much to mean that the layman is a priest as that the clergyman is not; "the priesthood of the Church" or "the priesthood of the Body" would be more accurate, and it is notable that the New Testament stresses this corporate aspect rather than the individual.[1] "He made us to be a kingdom, to be priests unto his God and Father"[2], it is true; but "ye are an elect race, a royal priesthood, a holy nation, a people for possession"[3], "ye also, as living stones, are built up a spiritual house, to be a holy priesthood"[4]—it is to the Church in its corporate aspect as Christ's body that his priesthood is communicated, and this communicated and corporate priesthood is seen in its fullest exercise when the Church is assembled together, with all its members playing their several and interrelated parts in one organic and coherent activity of praise and offering, for the celebration of the Eucharist, the rite which day by day recreates the Church and maintains its life. In this great priestly activity, centered in and flowing from the Eucharist but penetrating every aspect of human life, as Christ's members take him with them into their homes and into their daily work, men and women are united without differentiation of status. This priestly character is committed primarily to the Church as Christ's Body and only secondarily to its members as individuals, for it arises directly out of their incorporation into the Body at their baptism; in Christ there is neither Jew nor Greek, bond nor free, male nor female, for they are all one man in Christ Jesus.

---

[1] "The priesthood of the laity" can be given a legitimate sense if it is used to mean "the priesthood of the Church as exercised by the laity," or "the participation of the laity in the priesthood of the Church".
[2] Rev., i. 6; cf. v. 10.   [3] I Pet. ii. 9.   [4] ibid., ii. 5.

The priestly ministry

Together with this corporate participation in Christ's priesthood, which is communicated to the Church as a whole as his body, there is an individual participation in his priesthood, which is communicated to the Church's ministers. So far from the ministry being something contrived by the Church for its own convenience, it was instituted by Christ himself when he called twelve men to him and commissioned them to be his apostles. Indeed it would hardly be an exaggeration to say that it is clearer from the Gospels that he instituted a ministry than that he instituted a church; it is at least true that his way of founding a church was by founding a ministry and giving it an apostolic commission. "*Upon* this rock I will build my church"—not "independently of it"; and the Acts of the Apostles bears witness to the fact that the extension and establishment of the Church was a peculiarly apostolic function. I do not think that the argument which I am developing here is in any relevant respect affected by the variety of the views that are canvassed at the present day about the way in which the threefold ministry of the middle of the second century emerged from the "tunnel" which connects it with the New Testament. I think that Charles Gore was right in maintaining that "the New Testament appears definitely to exclude the possibility that the functions exclusively discharged by the general or apostolic order in the first days . . . lapsed altogether, so that the Church of the second century would, as it were, have re-developed an apostolic order of bishops from below"[1], but this is not central to my argument. The essential theological facts as I see them are these. Jesus is, as the Epistle to the Hebrews makes plain, both the Apostle and the High Priest of our confession[2], and both these offices are combined in his person in virtue of the fact that he is the incarnate Son of God. To the Church as his Body these offices are communicated. By participation in him the Church is both Apostle and High Priest; because the Whole Christ is Head and members together, Apostleship and Priesthood are united in the Body as they are united in the Head. It is indeed true, and it is central to our theme, that Christ's priesthood is not the levitical priesthood of the Old Dispensation. This

[1] *The Church and the Ministry*, new ed., p. 242.   [2] Heb. iii. 1.

again is made plain by the Epistle to the Hebrews: "It is evident that our Lord hath sprung out of Judah; as to which tribe Moses spake nothing concerning priests."[1] Nor does the sacrifice which he offers continue the line of the sacrifices of the Jewish law. He instituted his ritual sacrifice not by doing something to the sacrificial rites of the Old Dispensation but by giving a sacrificial character to a rite of thanksgiving for food and drink which previously was not in the strict sense sacrificial at all, by declaring that the cup at the Last Supper was the cup of the New Covenant in his blood. But this, so far from opposing his apostleship to his priesthood, makes his priesthood a consequence of his apostleship. It is because he is the Apostle, the one *sent* by the Father, that he is also the High Priest and the Victim. "A body didst thou prepare me . . . Then said I, Lo, I am come to do thy will, O God."[2] It is of the very essence of the New Covenant that in it apostleship and priesthood are united: in him as the Head, in the Church as his Body, in the ministry of the Church as his agent and as the Church's vital organ. But why, we may wonder, is there any need for a ministry at all?

If we may venture to speculate on the reason for this and to enquire why it was not sufficient for the welfare of Christ's members that they should simply be incorporated into his body by baptism and enjoy thereby their corporate participation in his apostleship and priesthood, we must presumably reply that Christ intended that future generations of his followers, no less than those who saw him in the days of his flesh, should come to God and live as children of God through the ministration of a person or persons. Dr. A. L. Peck has well emphasised the essentially *personal* nature of God's dealings with us in the Church; we are not baptised or absolved by "the ministry" but by *a minister*, not confirmed by "the episcopate" but by *a bishop*.

> We shall never see clearly what "the episcopate" is until we think of it in personal terms, until we realise that we are concerned not with an institution but with persons, until we realise that the bishop is the personal representative of the personal Christ, the vicarious father of the heavenly Father.[3]

The corporate priesthood of the whole Church is of course itself intensely personal, in the sense that the Church consists

---

[1] Heb. vii. 14.   [2] Cf. Heb. x. 5f.
[3] *This Church of Christ*, p. 36.

of persons, and nowhere is this seen more clearly than in the Eucharist. But the exercise of the priesthood by the Christian minister acting as such is personal, and indeed individual, in a quite different way; in his sacerdotal acts Christ's priesthood is, as it were, channelled or focused to a point and made operative through the words and gestures of one particular man, who blesses, absolves or presides at the Eucharist. It is this manifestation of Christ's priesthood with its inherent personal and individual character, and not that which is shared in by the Church as a whole, which the Church has limited to members of the male sex. What we have now to enquire is whether this limitation is—not deducible from (for we have seen that Christian theology does not proceed in a purely syllogistic way), but congruous with—the basic truths of the Christian religion.

Now when we consider the Christian priest as his essential status is manifested in his highest office as the celebrant of the Eucharist, it seems clear that he acts in the person of both God the Father and of the Lord Jesus Christ. St Ignatius of Antioch, writing at the beginning of the second century and interpreting the relation of the bishop to the Church in the light of his function as the normal celebrant of the Eucharist surrounded by his presbyters, wrote as follows to the Magnesians:

> Be ye zealous to do all things in godly concord, the presbyters after the likeness of the council of the Apostles, with the deacons also who are most dear to me, having been entrusted with the diaconate of Jesus Christ.[1]

And again:

> As the Lord did nothing without the Father (being united with him), either by himself or by the Apostles, so neither do ye anything without the bishop and presbyters.[2]

And to the Trallians:

> When ye are obedient to the bishop as to Jesus Christ, it is evident to me that ye are living not after men but after Jesus Christ . . . Be ye obedient also to the presbytery, as to the Apostles.[3]

And again, to the Smyrnaeans:

> Do ye all follow your bishop, as Jesus Christ followed

[1] Mag. 6. Cf. Trall. 3.   [2] Mag. 7.   [3] Trall. 2.

the Father, and the presbytery as the Apostles ... Wheresoever the bishop shall appear there let the people be, even as where Jesus Christ may be there is the universal Church.[1]

We need not be puzzled by the alternation between the Father and Christ as archetypes of the bishop's office. "He who hath seen me hath seen the Father,"[2] our Lord declared to Philip. "No man hath seen God at any time; the only begotten Son, which is in the bosom of the Father, he hath declared him."[3] And behind St Ignatius's language there is almost certainly the vision of the heavenly worship in the Apocalypse, seen as the inner reality of the Church's eucharistic rite, in which the central position is occupied both by the Father *upon* the throne and the Lamb "as it has been slain" *in the midst of* the throne, and in which the flanking figures of the four and twenty elders stand for the twelve Patriarchs of the Old Israel and those twelve Patriarchs of the New Israel who are the twelve Apostles called and commissioned by Christ, the supreme Apostle of the Father. And now that the presbyteral order has come to exercise the chief liturgical functions which in St Ignatius's letters belong to the bishop, it is the priest as the normal liturgical minister who is to be envisaged *ad instar Patris* and *ad instar Christi*. Now it is not, I think, a matter of chance that both the Father and the Son are denoted, both in Scripture and in Christian theology, by words of the masculine gender and never of the feminine. I do not suggest, of course, that there is in the triune Godhead anything crudely corresponding to the biological characteristic of sex, nor am I forgetful that in the book Genesis God is described as creating both man and woman in his own image: "God created man in his own image, in the image of God created he him; male and female created he them."[4] Nevertheless he created them in *his* own image, not in *hers;* and if it is suggested that the use of masculine terms is a mere accident of language or that the analogical application of terms to God is so remote that their gender is of no significance, it will, I think, be sufficient to remark that our belief in God would be different from what it is if the Trinity was described as consisting of Mother, Daughter and Spirit or if, taking refuge in terms of common gender, we described it as consisting of Parent, Offspring and Spirit simply. It is in no way derogatory to the female sex

[1] Smyrn. 8.   [2] John xiv. 9.   [3] John i. 18.   [4] Gen. i. 27.

to point out that the Christian priest is to exercise fatherhood and not motherhood to God's family, because his office is a participation in God's own relationship to his people, and God is our Father in heaven and not our Mother. The female sex has its own peculiar dignity, as we shall see in a moment; but we can hardly imagine it exercising the Fatherhood of God. And that God is the Father of his people is one of the dominant themes of Old and New Testament alike; in the Church, which is the New Israel and the Body of his Son, God's fatherhood is extended to Jew and Gentile indifferently.

When we consider the priest *ad instar Christi* the matter becomes even clearer, for here we are concerned not merely with the application of terms of human provenance to the Deity, but with the fact that the Second Person of the Holy Trinity has assumed a concrete human nature and has assumed it in the male sex. Christ, our High Priest, is a man (*anēr, vir*) and not a woman. Once again, if anyone is inclined to think that this is, theologically speaking, a mere accident, so that Christ might just as well have been born as a female child, it should be enough to suggest the mental exercise of substituting a female figure for the central figure of the Gospels and asking whether our religion would be substantially the same or radically different. Would it really make no difference to the Christian religion if it taught that God was a Trinity of Mother, Daughter and Spirit and that in the fulness of time, for us and for our salvation, the Daughter became a woman of a human father without the agency of a human mother? Is it not plain that the priesthood of Christ is, in no merely biological sense but in some profound and mysterious sense which lies behind and provides the ground of the biological differentiation, a male function, and can we doubt that this is the basis of our Lord's choice of men alone to be his Apostles and of the Church's instinctive sense that the *personal* exercise of the communicated and participated priestly office of Christ must be restricted to men?

Male and female in Christianity

The fact must be faced that the Church is the perpetuation on earth of the Incarnation, and that in the Incarnation the two sexes are involved in different ways; it is only to be expected that this difference will in some way be reflected in the structure and life of the Church. It was *male human nature* that the Son of God united to his divine person; it was a *female human person* who was chosen to be his mother. On the other hand, no *male human person* was chosen to be the Messiah (to suppose so was the error of the adoptionists), and no *female human nature* was assumed by a divine person. Thus from one point of view the Incarnation exalts the male sex above the female, while from another point of view it exalts the female sex above the male. In no woman has human *nature* been raised to the dignity which it possesses in Jesus of Nazareth, but to no male human *person* has there been given a dignity comparable to that which Mary enjoys as the Mother of God, a dignity which, in the words of the Eastern Orthodox Church, makes her "more honourable than the cherubim and beyond comparison more glorious than the seraphim". It may be worth noting that the discoveries of modern biological science have, if anything, enhanced rather than diminished the importance of Mary's part in the Incarnation, for, in contrast to the purely receptive role which Aristotelian biology ascribed to the mother in procreation, it presumably involves that the whole of our Lord's human genetic inheritance was derived from Mary. The fundamental fact about the two sexes is not that one is superior to the other, but that they are different. This difference is reflected both in the different roles that they play in the work of redemption, and in the different roles that they play in the economy of the Church. It is, I believe, the almost complete neglect of Mariology in the Church of England and in the Protestant Churches that has led to the demand that the functions of the two sexes in the Church shall be simply identical. As Mrs. Blomfield has profoundly remarked:

> The order of the laity is represented above all by women, for the simple reason that they cannot be priests. Certain actions are reserved to men in the Church, and we are told that it is because every man (a server, for example) is a potential priest. The reason is sufficient, but it is double-edged. It gives to woman a position among the laity which is all her own; it makes "the priesthood of the laity" pre-eminently hers. To understand how this may be, we must turn our eyes to the Queen of the Laity, Mary the Blessed Virgin.[1]

---

[1] op. cit., p. 37.

The question is sometimes raised, as by the Right Revd Glyn Simon in a letter in *Theology* of March 1955, whether in the Incarnation any difference of the sexes is not transcended. "'In Christ Jesus is neither male nor female'; not *man*hood but humanity was taken by the Word of God; human nature is neither male human nature nor female human nature; man *and* woman, neither alone, make up what we understand by human nature."[1] And it is often argued from considerations such as this that priesthood cannot be fully and adequately exercised in human nature unless it is exercised by persons of both sexes. The most careful distinctions are necessary here. In his first place, the text quoted from St Paul certainly does not mean that Jesus of Nazareth was not of the male sex, but that, in Christianity as contrasted with Judaism, women no less than men are incorporated into Christ by baptism and made sharers in the New Covenant of his blood. And the rest of the sentence—"Human nature is *neither* male human nature *nor* female human nature; man *and* woman, *neither alone*, make up what we understand by human nature"— seems to make two mutually contradictory statements, implying first that our Lord ought to be asexual and then that he ought to be hermaphrodite. The application to the doctrine of redemption of the assertion that "man and woman, neither alone, make up what we understand by human nature" has in fact been made use of in a very alarming way by some of the more extreme Roman Catholic Mariologists in order to argue that the Blessed Virgin has not merely a secondary but a primary part in the redemption of the human race; for, they hold, our Lord, being in his manhood male and not female, cannot without an equally primary co-operation on the part of a female human being, make a complete offering of human nature to the Father. It is surely necessary to hold that the exercise of priesthood by our Lord in the male sex does not in the least render incomplete the offering of universal human nature in consequence of the hypostatic union; and if this is so, there is no reason to suppose that the participation of that priesthood by the Church's ministers is in any way incomplete if there too it is exercised only in the male sex. Rather, this is what we should expect.

In a letter in *Theology* of January 1955 Miss M. E. Thrall raised the somewhat similar point that "the distinction between Jew and Gentile was to the Biblical writers of no less fundamental importance than the distinction between male

[1] loc. cit., p. 102.

and female" and that "if the selection of priests is to be determined by a consideration of the individual characteristics possessed by the human nature of Christ as a necessary consequence of the particularity of the Incarnation, we might equally well, on the face of it, argue that since the Word became man as a Jewish individual the Christian priesthood should be Jewish by birth."[1] Now this is on the surface a very plausible argument, so plausible indeed that we can hardly suppose that the primitive Church never thought of it. It is perfectly true that both the distinctions to which Miss Thrall refers are transcended in Christ, but it does not follow from this that they are transcended *in the same way*. If the primitive Church had thought so, it would no doubt have extended the priesthood to women as it did to Gentiles. If we wish to find out the precise ways in which the two distinctions are transcended, all we can do is to look at the practice of the primitive Church and see what light is cast upon it by the body of Christian doctrine as a whole; and this is what I have tried to do in the preceding discussion.

Furthermore, transcendence is not abolition. In spite of the fact that the distinction between Jew and Gentile is transcended in the Church, the Jew and the Gentile have different theological functions in the dispensation of God, as St Paul was at pains to make clear. So have men and women. And the distinction between Jew and Gentile is a different distinction from the distinction between man and woman, even though both distinctions are transcended without being abolished in the Christian Church. And therefore they are transcended in different ways.

Miss Thrall is at least to be complimented on the fact that she has attempted to approach the matter from a theological and not from a sentimental point of view. In an article which appeared in *Theology* in September 1954 and which was expanded into a short book, published under the title *The Ordination of Women to the Priesthood* in 1958, she makes a very thorough examination of the Biblical evidence. (In her book she remarks upon the theological inadequacy of the "feminist" arguments of such earlier advocates as Miss Edith Picton-Turbervill Canon C. E. Raven and Canon R. W. Howard.[2]). In her article, she argues at length that the notion of priesthood is closely connected with that of "dominion":

[1] loc. cit., p. 26.
[2] E. Picton-Turbervill *Should Women be Priests and Ministers?*, 1953; C. E. Raven, *Women and Holy Orders*; R. W. Howard, *Should Women be Priests?*, 1950.

> Man is a creature, and if he is to exercise dominion he must do so in accordance with the will of the Creator by whom it was given to him. He thus becomes the mediator of God's will and purpose to those over whom he rules, and he must in some sense continually offer his subjects and his realm in sacrifice to God, instead of considering them his own property.[1]

Miss Thrall then maintains, on the basis of a close examination of the early chapters of *Genesis*, that the dominion of the male over the female is a result of the fallen condition of the human race, and is properly reflected in the law of the Old Dispensation. But this, she contends, is done away in Christ, and therefore in the Christian Church women should be admitted as of right to the priesthood, since dominion is restored to woman equally with man in the New Dispensation. If Miss Thrall is correct, therefore, the Christian Church throughout its existence has had a grossly inadequate understanding of the effects of Christ's redemptive work; it has entirely failed to see one of the most important consequences of the restoration of the human race by Christ. As the Ven. G. F. Hilder remarked, in a comment upon Miss Thrall's article which does not seem to have been in any way rebutted in her book,

> Her argument, on its premises, is both lucid and cogent. But it starts from, and depends upon, the assumption that "dominion" is all of one kind—that represented by man's relationship to chattels in his possession—so that a subordinate state is necessarily servile. The passages of Scripture which have been taken to signify that man has been given by God in creation a certain primacy or headship over women are simply disregarded . . . The effect of this omission however is serious, as it goes to the root of the whole matter under discussion. It is clear that in the scriptural view there is a servile element in woman's status which is the consequence of sin, reflecting the servile state into which, from sonship, man himself has fallen. From both servitudes Christ has won redemption, though manifestly the outward effects of bondage are not in this life simply abolished. But just as man's fallen condition of servitude is the perversion of a creaturely state of filial dependence upon God, so it is at least possible that the fallen servitude of woman only

[1] art. cit., p. 331.

exaggerates, perverts and masks the true subordination to man which is her place in creation. In this case the proper meaning of that "headship" of man spoken by St Paul can be seen only in Christ, when the partnership of the sexes is freed from the false pattern of domination and servitude with which sin has overlaid it.[1]

Miss Thrall's omission to discuss the scriptural passages in question was, as the Archdeacon of Taunton recognised, to some extent repaired in an article by Dr. Sherwin Bailey which accompanied hers. But it can hardly be said to take the New Testament evidence seriously.

> Dr Bailey . . . frankly recognises that a "theory of subordination" appears in certain Pauline Epistles and in I Peter. But he regards this as merely a rationalisation of the social outlook of contemporary Judaism, supported in St Paul by a rabbinical exposition of the second creation story in Genesis ii. Similarly he argues that Genesis ii and iii are themselves to be regarded as a reflection in mythological form of woman's actual situation in the ancient world.[1]

Miss Thrall, in her book, takes a rather different line from this. She is not prepared to assert that the teaching of the New Testament writers about the status of women is sub-Christian in itself, nor, apparently, that St Paul failed to see the implications of his own doctrine. Attending particularly to the discussion in I Corinthians xi, she suggests that "the solution of the problem is perhaps to be found in the general situation of the Christians at Corinth,"[2] and that St Paul's attitude was governed by the peculiar circumstances of his day. The reason why he refused to tolerate the notion of women exercising the Christian ministry was that in the ancient world Christians were under a constant temptation to fall into idolatry, and that women, under the conditions of the Fall, had a particular leaning towards nature-mysticism and so were more prone to idolatry than men.

> The great danger, for the Gentile churches, was the temptation to slip back into the worship of the creature, and the women in particular would be subject to the temptation of idolatry. The worship of the one true God in Israel went hand in hand with the rigid subordination

[1] "Women and the Ministry", in *Theology*, December 1954, p. 453. [2] op. cit., p.74.

of women. The assertion and expression of monotheism in the Gentile communities of the New Israel required an equally strict subjection of the women to the authority of the men.[1]

However, Miss Thrall assures us, neither of these reasons which were so cogent in the first century is of force today.

Idolatry, in the strict sense of regarding the creation as an object of religious worship, is a thing of the past. The rise of the natural sciences has destroyed, even in the less well-educated sections of the population, any lingering belief that the universe is controlled by daemonic natural powers, and effectively prevents the ordinary man or woman from looking on natural phenomena with a feeling of numinous awe.

And,

as far as the Church is concerned, the education of women ought to mean that Christian women are able to realise to the full their redeemed existence in the Image of God. They are no longer subject to the temptation to indulge in what Brunner describes as "nature-mysticism". Consequently, there is no longer any need for their continued subordination.[2]

Both these views, I must confess, seem to me to be highly improbable. It is, one may suggest, at least as likely that Dr. Bailey has confused the social fashions and prejudices of his own day with the plain implications of the Christian religion as that the New Testament writers did the same thing with theirs. And Miss Thrall's argument seems to me to be a desperate expedient to save St Paul's face without accepting his conclusions. That he should have excluded one half of the Church's members from a status that had been restored to them by Christ, and this for no better reason than that they were somewhat more likely than the other half to succumb to a temptation which was constantly present to all and which, in any case, like other temptations was not irresistible in the power of Christ, is surely incredible, and Miss Thrall's bland assumption that the danger has been virtually abolished by the development of scientific civilisation and female education seems to me to show a sad declension from the theological

[1] ibid., p. 109. [2] ibid., p. 109, 111.

and realistic level on which her preceding arguments were conducted. It would follow from her interpretation that it is only in the more urbanised sections of the Anglo-Saxon world that women are now qualified for Holy Orders, and presumably that if a situation arose in which men were notably more prone to idolatry than women the Church would be right in excluding them from the priesthood in their turn. It is not really plausible that the very structure of the Church's ministry is meant to depend upon such purely contingent circumstances as these. And it should be noted that if the last part of her argument fails, not only does her conclusion not follow but much of her previous discussion weighs heavily against it.

Among modern Anglo-Saxons, with their uncritical sympathy with "democracy" and their impatience with any form of restraint (an impatience which is very understandably accentuated by the unnatural character of many of the restraints which the modern world imposes), the very word "subordination" tends to provoke a violent negative reaction. Nevertheless, in the strict etymological sense, *sub-ordination*, in the sense of the ordering of human beings under and over one another in accordance with the functions that they are called upon to perform, is a necessity of social life and can no more be dispensed with in the twentieth century than in the first; it rightly carries with it no suggestion of either arbitrariness, tyranny or exploitation. And in the matter with which we are here concerned any such suggestion is altogether excluded by the Pauline writings. In the eleventh chapter of the First Epistle to the Corinthians we are told that the head of the woman is the man, and the head of every man is Christ, and the head of Christ is God. This does not, of course, mean that in all the three cases headship is exercised in precisely the same way; to use the technical terms, "headship" is an analogical and not a univocal concept. But neither is it purely equivocal, or there would be no force in making the comparison. And if the headship of God over Christ is the archetype of both Christ's headship over the man and the man's headship over the woman, no implication of servile subjection is possible. The fundamental relation of Christ to the Father is not one of inferiority but of filiality and derived equality. The fundamental relation of the Christian man to Christ is not one of inferiority but of membership and reception of communicated sonship. And behind St Paul's thought about the man and the woman we must surely see the story of the creation of Eve from the side of Adam, in which the fundamental relation is not one of inferiority but of mutual perfection and of derived partnership: "I will make him a help meet for him."¹ The thought is carried even further in the magnificent sixth chapter of the Epistle to the Ephesians, in which husbands are exhorted to love their wives with that same self-giving love with which Christ loved the Church and gave himself for it. Throughout, superordination is manifested not in tyranny but in self-giving; subordination is manifested not is servility but in receptiveness and response. If women are incapable of receiving Holy Orders, it cannot be just because they are, in the vulgar sense of the word, *subordinate* to men, but because of the particular way in which masculinity and femininity are involved in the whole dispensation of redemption. Now I have already urged that the masculinity of the Christian priest is organically correlated with the masculinity of the great High Priest, whose priesthood is communicated to him and operates through him; and this contention is reinforced by the scriptural teaching that Christ's relation to the Church is the archetype — the supreme instance — of the relation of a husband to his wife. The fatherhood of God towards his people, the sponsal relation of Christ to his bride the Church — it does not seem fantastic to hold that, if these are the archetypal bases of the Christian priesthood, it is essentially male in its character.

No doubt there are truths about the way in which the male and female sexes are related in the mystery of redemption and in the life of the Church which are only now beginning to be fathomed, and they are bound to have their implications for the Church's ministry. But if we are wise we shall hold on faithfully to the order which the Church has inherited from its first beginnings and attempt in humility to deepen our understanding of it, rather than overturn it on the strength of contemporary fashions and half-thought-out speculations. The Anglican Churches have never failed to pride themselves on their faithfulness to Scripture and primitive practice and to condemn those bodies which have innovated upon the Church's faith and practice. It would be difficult to conceive a more drastic innovation than the extension of Holy Orders to women; for there can hardly be any aspect of the Church's practice which conforms more closely to the Vincentian canon *Semper, ubique et ab omnibus*, than the restriction of priesthood to the male sex.

¹ Gen. ii. 18.

Women and the Threefold Ministry

J. J. von Allmen (translated by C. D. W. Robinson)

[*Editor's note*

THIS is not the first time that Professor von Allmen has turned his pen to the subject of the ordination of women. An important article of his entitled 'Est-il légitime de consacrer des femmes au ministère pastoral?' appeared in *Verbum Caro*, vol. 17 (1963), pp. 5-28, and his present essay may be regarded as supplementing and updating his earlier one. The earlier article made the following points, among others:

1. That in this matter all is of grace: no one has a *right* to be ordained to the pastoral ministry, so the question of women's rights is irrelevant.

2. That the pastoral ministry is an institution of Christ, not an arrangement of convenience made by the Church, which can be altered at will.

3. That the doctrine of the priesthood of all believers is irrelevant. Ordination does not admit one to the priesthood of believers, nor does the withholding of ordination exclude one from it.

4. That women are definitely upgraded in the New Testament, and that this shows their continued exclusion from the pastoral ministry by the New Testament not to be simply a cultural hangover but to be deliberate.

Professor von Allmen's earlier article was written against his own church background, which is Presbyterian. In his present essay, which is the substance of a long letter in reply to an enquiry from Miss Christian Howard, he considers the question how the matter is affected by being transferred to a setting in which there are bishops, and the normal or essential ministry is considered to be the episcopal ministry, the presbyteral ministry being merely dependant. Of course, not all episcopal Churches do consider the episcopal ministry to be the normal or essential ministry, and the presbyteral ministry merely dependant. Many Anglicans and Lutherans, for example, hold that the episcopate derives from the presbyterate, not the reverse, and that NT limitations on women's ministry apply indirectly to the episcopate, but directly to the presbyterate.]

Three presuppositions: ministry and priesthood

MY REPLY IS BASED on three presuppositions. First, I am convinced that no one will solve the problem of ministries in general and of the ministry of women in particular by starting from the concept of priesthood; witness the almost desperate efforts of the expositors, both Roman Catholic and others, to explain why from post-apostolic times onwards it has been legitimate to speak of ministries in terms of priesthood when the New Testament does not do so—or does so only very rarely, as in Rom. 15: 16, for example, where the 'priestly service of the gospel' seems to be understood in the sense of the ministry of the evangelisation of the world by the Word (and baptism?) rather than in the sense of the ministry of the edification of the church by the eucharist. On the whole, the New Testament makes use of the category of the 'apostolate' and that of 'ministry' (which usually covers the function of bishop, teacher, pastor, presbyter, deacon etc.). The question seems to me not to be: *Is it legitimate to ordain women to the priesthood?*, but rather: *To which ministry is it legitimate to ordain women?* It must be said again and again that neither the indispensability of the ministry for the church, nor its institution by the Lord, is endangered by refusing to understand it in terms of 'priesthood'. Ministry is not sacramental because it is priestly, but because it is apostolic.

My second presupposition is that the tradition of the church must be given decisive weight: it has known from very ancient times three regular ministries: the episcopate, a major ministry of apostolic succession; the presbyterate, a collegiate ministry participating in the episcopal ministry; and the diaconate, also a ministry participating in the episcopal ministry, though in a more personal way. I am aware that this raises many historical questions, some of which have not been solved and doubtless never will be. One point, however, seems to be clear: these three ministries are distinct from each other not only by the tasks which they entail, but also by the necessity that each should have its own proper 'legitimation'. There is a legitimation peculiar to the episcopate, another peculiar to the presbyterate, a third peculiar to the diaconate. One other point also seems clear: it is the episcopal ministry which, of the three, by very ancient tradition carries the most weight. To attest its ecclesial character a local church, for example, does not point to its presbyteral college, and still less to the presence, in its midst, of deacons: it points to its bishop. It is he who, at the level of ministry, certifies a church to be a church. That is why one finds early on that a particular church, when providing a successor to a deceased bishop, appoints one of its deacons or (later?) a member of its presbyterate, whereas one does not see a bishop becoming a presbyter or a deacon. Of course, the few historical exceptions which one always manages to unearth if one tries would have to be carefully weighed: but such exceptions would in fact only confirm the rule.

Sociological forms of the traditional ministry

THE last of the presuppositions, which constitute the basis of my argument, is that in the course of history there have been many structural or sociological variants by which this traditional scheme of ministry has been expressed, and that these variants have not necessarily compromised the faithfulness of those churches which adapted their own ministerial structure, as well as they could, to new conditions of place and time in which they were called to remain faithful as a church. The history of the presbyterate is particularly instructive in this respect, as is also the history of the relationship of precedence and prestige between the presbyterate and the diaconate, or that of the extent of presbyteral participation in the bishop's ministry. Because of historical vicissitudes, the faithfulness of a church lies not so much in perpetuating unconditionally a given sociological solution, adopted (to provide a framework for the relationship between bishop, presbyters and deacons) at a given time and in given circumstances. Faithfulness seems, rather, to depend on the two following factors: firstly, on the fearless desire to receive, practise and transmit faithfully the ministry of apostolic succession instituted by Christ and essential to the very existence of the church (the 'episcopal' ministry); secondly, on the flexibility and readiness necessary in order to adapt particularly the form of the presbyteral and diaconal ministries to the circumstances and needs of the church at a particular place and time, or in particular difficulties which it encounters in the course of its history. To take an example relating directly to the *Eglise Réformée* in which I was ordained: the Reformers were convinced on theological grounds that their rejection of the diocesan structure which distinguished a church from a parish—rejection not because of doctrinal stubbornness, but because the titular bishops of churches either would not hear of reform or seemed unconcerned about their church, giving it into the care of a suffragan—was not a rejection of the church structure required by the nature of the church, but merely of one *sociological* form which the structure can take. This conviction was due in large part to St. Jerome, whose hypothesis of the origin of the episcopate they had adopted, along with most of their contemporaries: according to him, the creation of the episcopate was a measure not of Messianic institution but of ecclesiastical law, a measure taken to strengthen the unity of the church by providing a structure for the presbyterate, itself recognised as the original ministry of apostolic succession.

They were convinced that theologically it is not possible to draw a meaningful distinction between bishops and presbyters, since both are ministries of the word, the sacraments and the 'keys' (discipline and absolution). The distinction being purely sociological, it was therefore possible, in the view of the Reformers, to avoid interrupting the necessary apostolic succession, while rejecting the 'episcopal' form of the essential ministry, so as to transfer it to and practise it at the level of the parish rather than the diocese, i.e. at the presbyteral level. (It is interesting to note that the term chosen for him who has this ministry was 'pastor', cognate with 'episcopal', rather than 'presbyter' = priest.) Thus, theologically, the equivalent of the 'reformed' pastor is not the 'catholic' presbyter (who is sociologically his peer), but the 'catholic' bishop (who is sociologically his superior). I have gone into detail about this in my book: *Le saint ministère selon la conviction et la volonté des réformés du XVIe siècle* [Neuchâtel, 1968], the fruit of thirteen years' research. This research has led me to distinguish the (variable) sociology of the church's structure from its (apostolic and so constant) theology. I am myself hesitant about following St. Jerome's way of presenting the origin of the episcopate. I must, however, say that my church—far from deliberately breaking with the current tradition, but rather basing its actions on belief in what St. Jerome and many other Fathers and Doctors affirmed—was convinced that it was upholding faithfully the ministry of apostolic succession instituted by Christ to gather together and edify his church until his return, since the succession of ordinations maintains the ministry of the Word, the sacraments and the 'keys'. It was also held that there was no reason to qualify or disqualify the church in and for which this ministry was exercised because of the sociological level at which it took place. This has had the following interesting and perhaps illuminating consequence for ecclesiology in general: in the *Eglise Réformée*, in Switzerland at least, the ordained ministry has been so reduced to a merely *pastoral* ministry that the relative status of the ministry of elders and deacons has become uncertain; indirectly, this provides proof that the faithfulness of a church depends not on these ministries, their ordination or the kind or degree of participation in the essential episcopal ministry that they have, but solely on the essential ministry.

This lengthy introduction was necessary to show how I approach the problem of the ordination of women to one of the traditional ministries of the church. Basically, and in principle, I stand by what I wrote in 'Est-il légitime de consacrer des femmes au ministère pastoral?' [*Verbum Caro*, 1963, a study reproduced in *Prophétisme sacramentel*, Neuchâtel, 1964]. Nevertheless, in view of subsequent literature I need to temper some arguments and strengthen others.

Three questions: women as bishops?

ATTEMPTING to transport myself in spirit to the Anglican situation, I see three questions which the Church of England has to face.

1. **Is it legitimate to ordain a woman to the episcopal ministry, i.e. to the ministry of apostolic succession which is essential to the church?** This is the question which faces you and which for us would be that of the ordination of women to the pastoral ministry. I start from the presupposition that the bishop is not a presbyter plus, but that he fulfils a ministry *sui generis* to which one must be specially ordained or consecrated in order to exercise it. In other words the difference between deacon, presbyter and bishop is of a different kind from that which distinguishes a bishop from an archbishop, a patriarch or the pope—a difference which (happily or not) exists within the hierarchy of the *same* episcopal ministry: the pope of Rome receives no higher degree of ordination to his ministry, if he is already ordained to the episcopate, than the archbishop of Canterbury, if he is already a bishop: both are *installed*, in all solemnity, to exercise their 'power of jurisdiction' in a new way.

Is it then legitimate to ordain a woman to the episcopal ministry? To this first question I answer in the negative. An affirmative reply would entail a twofold *theological* error, irrespective of the entirely different question whether such action would be politic or expedient.

The first error is ecclesiological, for it presupposes that the ministry is at bottom hardly more than a sociological measure necessary to the *bene esse* of the church, which, being a social body, needs officials. What would then prevent the recruitment of such officials by following the recruitment pattern of other social bodies? In a historical situation where officials for the other social bodies are recruited without the distinction between men and women being a deciding factor, if such a distinction is particularly unpopular with those who look forward rather than back, why should not the church adopt the same principles of selection as other social bodies, principles which ignore the natural distinction between men and women? I would go further: what, apart from an injurious attitude towards women, would prevent the opening of the most responsible tasks of the social body in question to women worthy and capable of them?

Theology and sociology

IT is clear that ecclesiology must involve sociological considerations. It is also clear that these considerations will be of particular importance in examining the application of doctrines of the ministry. The church is not, however, solely a social body: it is a mystery of salvation. The ministers are not merely officials of the church; they are witnesses and bearers of the very presence of Christ, they have a sacramental and not merely a sociological basis. An attempt to solve the problem by adopting a solution in fundamental conformity to the present age (cf. Rom. 12: 2) would be an admission, contrary to unanimous ecclesiastical tradition, that the ministry of apostolic succession is based, essentially, on the sociological needs of the church, and that these needs are more important than Christ's institution of it.

The reply will be made that the ordination of a woman to the ministry of apostolic succession does not necessarily indicate the reduction of what is a mystery of salvation to pure sociology: without affecting the nature of this ministry one could confer it on women as well as men. The only difference would be the rejection of an outdated custom which says that there is a real distinction between men and women and that duties and rights should be withheld from women which have until now been the privilege of men alone. It is not impossible to make out a case on these lines, and this is why a rejection of the ordination of women to the essential ministry which is based solely on ecclesiological considerations cannot suffice. Indeed, the objector will continue, since in Christ there is neither male nor female (Gal. 3: 28), it should be possible to confer this essential ministry on women as well as men without affecting its nature, particularly if society has changed its attitude on the role of women in society, and if one succeeds in showing that Jesus's not having chosen a woman as one of the twelve, or the church's not having replaced Judas by a woman, was due not to the lack of women able to fulfil the requirements (there must have been as many women as men able to do this!), but to prejudice or cautiousness, from which we have gradually freed ourselves by the light of the gospel. But *is* it only a question of prejudice? For me the question does not depend for its solution on sociological considerations but, in the last analysis, on the commitment of faith: human beings are not men and women by the accidental demands of reproduction, but are one or the other as part of their vocation, to the very depths of their being. Masculinity or femininity is a basic constituent of the human being, whether man or woman. This introduces the truly theological aspect of the problem: there are no grounds for believing that Jesus ceased to be Son by his resurrection. In this respect, I note that Paul in 1 Cor. 6: 12-20 relates sexual sins to the *resurrection* body. I note that it is not only for reasons of decency that the church has never considered turning homosexual relationships into marriage and giving them its blessing as being such. I note also the teaching on marriage in Ephesians 5: the writer states that there is between man and woman in marriage a relationship which ought to reflect that which unites Christ and the church—the man in Christ's position, the woman in that of the church. Christ and the church are not interchangeable. In short (and this seems to be a lesson from the history of heresies in the ancient church) one contradicts the doctrine of creation and with it biblical anthropology if one does not respect the ontological nature of masculinity and femininity. The fact that males, in their pride and egoism, have been guilty of abusing the distinction, is no reason to reduce the distinction to anything less than a profound, inalienable characteristic of man or woman. Sexuality cannot be reduced to a reproductive mechanism; if it were, against the mainstream of recent works on marriage, one would be obliged to admit that the sole justification of marriage is to provide the normal framework for the ordered reproduction of the human race.

In short, if women as well as men can be ordained to the essential ministry, to the ministry by which Christ makes himself publicly present to the church and to the world, then by implication, on the theological level, in Christian anthropology the polarisation of human beings by sexuality is not a constitutive characteristic of man or woman. Perhaps one could sum up by saying that God's eternal Son was not made man rather than woman simply in order to bow to a cultural prejudice. There is urgent need to realise that the ordination of men rather than women to the essential ministry in which, ordinarily and publicly, Christ is present to the church and to the world, is not a privilege which denies a right to women. Ministry is never a right. It is always a grace, not only for the minister, but also for the church and the world.

I am the first to recognise that only those already persuaded will be convinced by this line of argument. But I would like those unconvinced to answer these objections to the ordination of women as bishops. They should tell us in what respect they are not 'conforming to this present age' by wanting to recruit for the church in the same way as for other bodies in society; they should give us their reasons for questioning the anthropology of Marcion or Montanus—and with it their doctrine of creation; they should say why they regard human sexuality merely as a means of reproduction or as a plaything which does not go to the very depth of one's being; they should state why Mary's child could just as well have been a girl as a boy; they should explain how to remove the quality of *representatio Christi* from the essential ministry of the church without making it something different.

Women in the dependant ministries?

2. Other ministers may share in the episcopal ministry: can women then share in it? First, note that, in accordance with New Testament teaching, the episcopal ministry is not the only ministry in the church, even if it is the only ministry essential to the church. It is a ministry in which the bearer may invite others to join, as Moses had others help him in a task which was too much for him alone (cf. Exod. 18: 13-26), as the twelve enlisted the help of the seven in order to concentrate on the most important aspect of their ministry (Acts 6: 1-6), as Paul had Timothy, Titus, Silvanus etc. for fellow-workers. One of the best things in that fine third chapter of *Lumen gentium* adopted by Vatican II (if one puts brackets round its ponderous and frequent reference to the singularity of the ministry of the bishop of Rome) is the statement that the episcopal ministry is founded on the apostles' ministry, which it perpetuates, and that it is a ministry in which the other ministries which the church needs participate. Traditionally there are two such ministries: that of the presbyteral college and that of deacons. The question is this: may women be ordained either to the collegiate ministry of the presbyterate, or as deacons?

Over the centuries the participation of presbyters and deacons in the episcopal ministry has had various forms, proof that such participation is not bound to one rigid structure. Two examples: in the East it is traditional that a presbyter receives the right to confirm with the right to baptise, whereas in the West, traditionally, the bishop alone reserves the right to confirm; in the West the right of absolution is ordinarily part of the presbyteral ministry, whereas in the East, if I am informed correctly, this right is not so tightly linked with the presbyterate, since it can either not be conferred at the same time as presbyteral authority to preside at the eucharist, or can, exceptionally, be conferred on a 'staretz' or senior monk who is not a presbyter.

Note also, from the fourth century on, the growth of the system which, in order to avoid a piecemeal church, forbids the number of churches and so of bishops to equal the number of local congregations. This made small congregations *parishes* of the bishop's see, of the church. It entailed the dispersal of the college of presbyters and made their participation in most of the episcopal functions dependent upon the same relationship between presbyter and bishop as exists between the parish and the church. This system—roughly sketched— is rightly questioned at present as the *sole* system for the structure of the *local* church. Indeed, the participation of congregations in the life of the cathedral church can no longer be based solely on geographical factors in a society where social and residential stability and the fund of common interests are not so great as in a pre-industrial society. This is why in many places people demand that the church-parish relationship be reviewed, made more flexible and recast for the new situations of contemporary society. However, the abandonment of the geographical church-parish system as almost the only form of ecclesial participation would involve a serious review of the distribution of the participation of presbyters and deacons in the episcopal ministry; more diversity may grow up in the ways in which the service of presbyters and deacons is 'inserted' in their bishop's ministry; a presbyter will no longer be 'almost a bishop' because he heads what is 'almost a church', and a deacon will no longer be a man eager to become a presbyter. At the present time we have the chance—

similar to the opportunity in the fourth century, though different solutions will be needed—to rethink the way in which those other than bishops can be associated and integrated into the episcopal ministry.

Women as presbyters?

MAY women then be linked with the episcopal ministry by ordination as presbyters? Given that the sort of participation by presbyters in the episcopal ministry would be reviewed, would become less uniform and better adapted to the vocation and gifts of those fulfilling this ministry—given, in consequence, that the task of presbyter would no longer be to represent the bishop and, in him, Christ, at the head of a parish, and that the task would be determined specifically *ad personam* (and why not also *ad tempus*?) on the occasion of the ordination or the installation in new responsibilities, I can see no decisive theological reason to deny membership, by ordination, of the college of presbyters to women. I can, however, see two objections which must be taken seriously.

First, two of the traditional presbyteral tasks which are right in principle would probably not be included in a presbyterate in which women could be associated with the ministry of the bishop: the representation of the bishop, and in him of Christ, at the head of a parochial congregation (parishes will probably continue to exist for a long time alongside new forms of local church congregation), and the representation of the bishop and in him of Christ at the head of the eucharistic assembly (except perhaps in a female community). The tasks *ad personam* which would be given to women in the presbyterate would above all be the homiletic, catechetic and charitable responsibilities of the bishop. As a result, there would certainly be a sense of frustration among female presbyters, since they would not be candidates for a vacant episcopal see.

The second objection is that the tasks which would fall to female presbyters are those which have traditionally belonged to the diaconate. (I myself am very hesitant in subscribing to the idea that access to the ministry of the sacraments should be more closely guarded than to the ministry of the Word, but I see that tradition, even in the *Eglise Réformée*, has taken this line.) Consequently, it seems to me that it would be better to restore a diaconate which would not be simply a path to the presbyterate, but a ministry received as a grace in itself and for its own sake. What makes the church's acceptance of the vocations which the Lord had doubtless given to women a mockery is not the acceptance of women into the diaconate, but into a diaconate which is the *lowest* echelon in the hierarchy of ministries and which men rush to leave behind. If the diaconate could be once again a ministry of participation in the episcopate parallel to the presbyterate, if its tasks and rights were put on a higher level, as a diaconate to which not only women but men would be ordained for life, I believe that, without leaving the bounds of authentic tradition, the church would have taken an important step towards the abolition of a discrimination which is insulting to women and ungrateful towards God.

I would thus answer the second question in the affirmative, but with a marked preference for the ordination of women to a recast diaconate rather than to the presbyterate (even recast).

Ecumenically expedient?

3. The third question is this: **is it wise to settle the question of the ordination of women in the present ecumenical climate?**

Clearly the answer is yes if it is ordination to a diaconate enjoying the respect which the church owes to God's graces. But if (as one must fear) the problem presents itself in terms of the entry of women into the priesthood, if the question of the ordination of women to the episcopal ministry is excluded in principle from the discussion, if the parish structure of the church is barely examined, if the diaconate does not rediscover its autonomy over against the presbyterate—in short, if it is simply a question of having, in the traditional way, female priests alongside male priests—are you to proceed?

If you do, you will strengthen the vital contact with churches ecclesiologically 'left' of the Church of England and you will no doubt facilitate discussions on organic union with them. If you permit me to be completely frank about a church which I love, this contact is indispensable if you are to avoid a disturbing ecclesial anemia. I know only too well how ecclesiologically equivocal some 'evangelical' Christianity is. But it does have one major point in its favour: it always points to Jesus Christ, dead and risen, and we all continually need to come back there. . . .

If you do not proceed, you will strengthen the vital contact with churches ecclesiologically further to the 'right' than the Church of England. (By churches 'to the right' or 'to the left' I do not so much mean church people, for whom dividing lines between left and right are no longer denominational, I mean rather their leaders and representatives on whom, whether one likes it or not, the real decisions depend.) Is this contact, in the present situation, as important to you as the contact on your left? Indubitably so, if this contact is with the Roman Catholicism which breathes the clear air of Vatican II. I would be less certain if this contact is with the Roman Catholicism which is carried away by every new wind of doctrine or with the Roman Catholicism which mourns the time when Trent and Vatican I reigned unchallenged. Regretfully, I would be less certain, too, if this contact were with Eastern Orthodoxy, which presents itself, unfortunately, so much more willingly as that which we ought to desire to be, than as a partner in a common return to our sources in the ecclesial consciousness of the Fathers.

If a truly universal council were around the corner, I would say no to the third question which your church faces. It would be for the council to study in depth this problem and to find a solution acceptable to all.

Four considerations

BUT since this council is not in the offing, I would like to think that your church will follow these four pieces of advice:

1. Whatever solution is adopted, regard it as a specifically denominational solution rather than as a universal one, and so leave the way open for a re-examination of the problem and its solution when a truly universal council is held.

2. Do not let the ministry to which women are ordained be that of bishop: let it not be the ministry which traditionally (as I see it, rightly) is constitutive of the ecclesiality of a church, because constitutive of the church itself: let it be one of the two other ministries which participate in the episcopate.

3. Upgrade the diaconal ministry sufficiently to allow for women who have the calling to serve God by proclaiming the gospel to the world and edifying the church, to be received not suspiciously and meanly, but respectfully and generously. In other words, abandon the idea that the diaconate is above all a ministry which opens the way to the presbyterate, and insist on the theological identity between the diaconal ministry of men and that of women.

4. If, however, the ordination of women to the ministry of presbyter seems the only equitable solution, make sure first that it is clearly understood that the presbyteral ministry is a ministry of participation in the episcopal ministry, and that the latter is apostolic rather than sacerdotal in nature. In this way, remove from the start the link between the presbyterate and the priesthood, a link which has given rise to so many misunderstandings in the church. Make it clear that the priestly aspect which characterises every authentic ministry is secondary, derived, illustrative, and that it is not this priestliness which makes the ministry constitutive of the church, but rather its insertion (directly, in the case of the bishop's ministry, indirectly, in the cases of the ministries of presbyters and deacons) in the apostolic ministry instituted by Christ.

Towards a Better Solution

R. T. BECKWITH AND G. E. DUFFIELD

IN THESE ESSAYS, writers from five different countries, belonging to the Lutheran, Presbyterian and Anglican Churches, some of them Evangelical in their leanings and some Catholic, have considered the question of the ordination of women from the biblical, the theological and the historical points of view. They have concluded, with essential unanimity, that the ordination of women to the episcopate or presbyterate is a historical novelty (R. T. Beckwith), arising in part at least out of a modern secular cult (G. E. Duffield); that it is excluded by the teaching of the New Testament (G. G. Blum), a fact which is made more significant by the manifest willingness of our Lord and St. Paul to raise the status of women in other respects (esp. H. Cavallin), and by the actual existence of female ministers in the Greco-Roman religions and among the early heretics (E. R. Hardy); they have further concluded that the support which protagonists of the ordination of women claim to find in the Bible is read *into* the text not *out of* it, by selective and subjective methods of exegesis (H. Cavallin); and that the campaign for ordination is in radical conflict with Catholic theology (M. Bruce, E. L. Mascall), Presbyterian theology (J. J. von Allmen) and Evangelical theology (J. I. Packer).

If the case made out seems impressive, some may wonder, even so, whether it could not have been made more impressive still by the inclusion of contributions from Roman Catholic and Orthodox writers, and from women writers. The Roman Catholic[1] and Orthodox Churches are firmly opposed to the ordination of women, and some of the strongest opponents in all Churches are themselves women. But if it had been possible to include all the material submitted for use in this symposium, there would have been two Roman Catholic contributions, two Orthodox contributions, and five contributions by women. To avoid excessive length and going into details about particular denominations, it was necessary to exclude some items, but several of those not included supplied valuable material which is utilised elsewhere.

Theological principles and present debate

THE authors of the book have sought to judge the question before them on theological grounds. They remain unimpressed by the current attempt to settle the matter on grounds of sex discrimination. To refuse the priesthood to women, so it is said, is 'an inhuman act of discrimination' which 'disenfranchises half the human race from the liberation' brought by the gospel.[2] This is the way the matter is put from within the Church. From outside, the cry is that the London Stock Exchange and the Church are the two great bastions still remaining of sex discrimination in Britain. The decision of the Stock Exchange Council on May 2nd 1972 to admit women will only vary the slogan, but should make it progressively clearer to most people that what influences those within the Church who oppose the ordination of women to the priesthood is not secular convention but theological principle.

The idea that women will never have their full human rights until they are treated in all respects as if they were not women but men has unfortunately made considerable headway in the Church. Despite the reasoned opposition of Christian leaders and thinkers like Hensley Henson, William Temple, K. E. Kirk and C. S. Lewis, the campaign for the ordination of women to the priesthood continues to make some progress. The progress made is often exaggerated, however. Between the two surveys of member-churches carried out by the World Council of Churches in 1958 and 1970, the number of Churches ordaining women rose from 48 to about 70, but as the total number of member-churches in the same period rose from 168 to 239, the proportion was hardly affected, and it is difficult to say whether it was really a case of Churches that used not to ordain women changing their practice, or simply of Churches that ordain women joining the World Council. Some member-churches are known to have changed their practice during the period concerned, but not very many, and the Churches that do not ordain women still outnumber the Churches that do by two to one.

After the crisis among the Lutherans around 1960, the matter is now coming to a head again among Anglicans. It last did so in 1944, when the Bishop of Hong Kong ordained a deaconess to the priesthood, because he could see no other way of making the Lord's Supper available to a community isolated by war-time conditions. His action incurred the disapproval of the other bishops of China, of the 1948 Lambeth Conference and of Archbishop William Temple, who in a letter to the *Church Times* editor (quoted in that journal on November 26th 1971) said that the Bishop of Hong Kong should rather have authorised the deaconess to celebrate holy communion as a deaconess for the period of the emergency. In the circumstances, the deaconess resigned her priest's orders and returned to diaconal work.

In 1967, the National Assembly of the Church of England formally voted against the ordination of women to the priesthood, and the Lambeth Conference of the following year refused to be pressed into a contrary decision, but instead asked all provinces of the Anglican Communion to study the question and report their decision (resolution 35), a request repeated by the Anglican Consultative Council in 1971 (resolution 28a). In response to these requests, the General Convention of the Protestant Episcopal Church in the U.S.A. voted in 1970 against having women priests, and in 1972 the General Synod of the Church of the Province of New Zealand also voted against having them. Only the Church of the Province of Burma has so far voted (simply in principle) the other way. However, the diocese of Hong Kong, now under a new bishop, has once again gone ahead on its own. This time, the bishop first applied to the Anglican Consultative Council for advice, and received advice, by a majority of 24 to 22, that

> if he decides to ordain women to the priesthood, his action will be acceptable to this Council; and that this Council will use its good offices to encourage all Provinces of the Anglican Communion to continue in communion with these dioceses [i.e. Hong Kong and any that might act similarly (resolution 28b)].

This advice evoked stern editorial comment even in the secular press, and E. L. Mascall wrote of it

> A majority of 2 votes in an assembly of 46 only shows that the Council had really no advice to give. . . . No one would hang a cat on such a vote as this; is it sufficient to justify the abandonment of the historic tradition of Christendom?[3]

The Council of the Church of South East Asia (Hong Kong's only quasi-provincial link, now that mainland China is under Communist control) desired the bishop to hold his hand, but he declined. In November 1971 he ordained two deaconesses to the priesthood.

Even if these purported ordinations are accepted at their face value, they undoubtedly lack almost entirely the present *catholicity* of Anglican orders. As things stand, Anglican clergy are free to move from province to province, and to exercise their orders wherever they go, provided they can conscientiously conform to the local provincial regulations. The two women priests from Hong Kong will have no such freedom. A province which has decided against changing its regulations so as to allow the ordination of women priests at home is certainly not going to change its regulations so as to allow the institution or licensing of women priests from abroad. Consequently, if other provinces of the Anglican Communion decide as PECUSA and New Zealand have done, the women priests of Hong Kong bid fair to be frozen in that diocese. It would have been kinder of the Anglican Consultative Council to have given Hong Kong this warning, separated as it already is from the rest of the province of China, rather than to have buoyed it up with delusive hopes of world wide 'communion', which could only mean something very different from what 'communion' has meant to Anglicans hitherto. In the event, the two Hong Kong women priests, like their predecessor, may well find it necessary to resign their orders. Alternatively, they may live out their days as isolated oddities in the Anglican Communion, and leave no successors. It seems hard that two successive Bishops of Hong Kong should subject their women workers to this kind of guinea-pig treatment. One does not know whom to envy less, the women priests of Hong Kong, with their precarious future, or the non-Anglican women ministers who simply ceased to be ministers because of the inauguration of the united Church of North India in 1970.[4]

In the Church of England, another vote on the ordination of women is intended, perhaps because the vote of 1967 was taken before the Lambeth Conference and the Anglican Consultative Council made their requests for a consideration of the matter. To this end, Miss Christian Howard has prepared for the Advisory Council on the Church's Ministry a report entitled *The Ordination of Women to the Priesthood: a Consultative Document*.[5] This report is valuable for the information it contains, and does not ignore theological considerations, even if in places it approaches theology in that unbiblical and agnostic manner which is exemplified in the preface to the ill-omened report of the Anglican Consultative Council: 'There was no option but to try to play into the hands of the Holy Spirit. The problem, then, is how to test for what the Spirit wants' (*The Time is Now*, London, SPCK, 1971, p. ix).

Evasions of theology

AS the debate in the Church of England and the rest of the Anglican Communion develops, it is to be hoped that theological considerations will at last be given their due place, and that the popular evasions of the theological case will be carefully scrutinised and be found to be what they really are, evasions. Thus, we shall no doubt be hearing once more that in Christ there can be neither Jew nor Greek, bond nor free, male nor female (Gal. 3: 28).[6] But the preceding verse makes it perfectly clear that the context of this statement is baptism, so the meaning is that all these classes equally can enter the Church and find salvation. Elsewhere, Paul takes each of the three groups, and shows that under the Christian gospel the distinctive roles of Jew and Gentile are not abolished (Rom. 1: 16; 2: 9f.; 11: 11-32), nor are the distinctive roles of bond and free abolished (1 Cor. 7: 20-24; Eph. 6: 5-9; Col. 3: 22-4: 1), any more than the distinctive roles of male and female are.

This answer at once gives rise to a second evasion: slavery has now been abolished, we are reminded, and with it the distinctive roles of bond and free. Why, then, should the distinctive roles of male and female be regarded as having any greater permanence?[7] Here there are two points to be made. The first is that slavery is a purely adventitious relationship, whereas sex is grounded in human nature. The second is that Paul regarded the distinctive roles of bond and free as remaining for as long as the institution within which they were exercised (i.e. slavery) remained. He may have looked forward to the abolition of slavery: he certainly did not regard the lot of the slave as a very desirable one (1 Cor. 7: 21, 23), any more than the Old Testament did (Lev. 25: 39-55), but what he did not look forward to was masters and slaves, *within the institution of slavery*, renouncing their duties to one another. On the contrary, he insisted that as long as the institution of slavery remained, the roles and duties of the two parties within it also remained. Now, by parity of reasoning, one could not abolish the distinctive roles and duties of male and female without first abolishing those institutions, such as the family and the congregation, in which these roles and duties have to be exercised. But to abolish the family would be to abolish one of the ordinances of creation, and to abolish the congregation would be to abolish the Church of Christ.

Once again, the evasion is no sooner answered than another takes its place. The third evasion claims that the headship of the man is a relationship which does not exist outside the family, and that when the New Testament applies the relationship to the congregation, it is only concerned with the relationship of wives to their own husbands within it. But one such passage is 1 Cor. 11: 2-16, where 'woman' covers a man's mother as well as his wife (v. 12). The discussion of veiling in the passage is also significant, for it seems to have been the Jewish custom that virgins and widows as well as wives should veil themselves.[8] Another such passage is 1 Tim. 2: 8-15, where 'men' and 'women' in the opening two verses appear to cover everyone in the congregation, married or single. Moreover, as Bishop Kirk points out,[9] if the headship of the man in the congregation is rejected, his headship in the family will be gravely imperilled. How could the headship of a husband in his family be unaffected, if his own wife was ordained to headship in the congregation to which he belonged; or (supposing he was in orders himself) if his wife were appointed rector and he assistant curate, or his wife bishop and he rector? Indeed, even if a case where the wife was not herself ordained, she would be sorely tempted to arrogate to herself a position in the family equal or superior to the headship over her husband exercised in the congregation by some other woman. Besides, it is difficult to see what this evasion achieves, for those who urge it usually object to the headship of the man in the family as much as in the congregation, and often object to all headship and subordination, in every realm of life.[10]

A fourth evasion that is regularly heard is that Paul contradicts himself and therefore cannot be our guide. Whatever he may say in 1 Cor. 14 and 1 Tim. 2, we are told, in 1 Cor. 11: 5 he does not regard it as contrary to a due subordination that a woman should prophesy or lead in prayer, only that she should do it unveiled. This is a dubious inference, as is pointed out elsewhere. From other passages, we can be sure that Paul would not try to quench the gift of prophecy (1 Cor. 14; 1 Thes. 5: 19f.), but his subject in 1 Cor. 11 is not women's ministry but women's dress. If it was when prophesying and leading in prayer that Corinthian women removed their veils, Paul would naturally say so, but without thereby implying any judgment on these side-issues. There is therefore no reason to think that the passage authorises the women of Corinth to lead in prayer, especially as ch. 14, vv. 33-36, and 1 Tim. 2: 8ff. seem to forbid it. If the objection comes back that Paul admittedly allowed women to prophesy, and prophecy is very much the same thing as the presbyter's work of teaching, the reply must be that it is not. The New Testament prophet, unlike the presbyter, had no human commission and no pastoral cure. He received direct revelations from God (1 Cor. 14: 30; Eph. 3: 2-5), predicted the future (Acts 11: 28; 21: 11; Rev. 1: 3, 19; 4: 1) and in other ways acted like the prophets of the Old Testament, performing symbolic revelatory acts and wandering from place to place under the leading of the Spirit (Acts 11: 27; 21: 10f.). His spiritual gift was comparable to that of the apostle (Eph. 2: 20; 3: 5), and was an expression of the freedom of the Spirit to breathe where he will, and to show himself not bound (except where he so desires) by the rules that he makes for us. Thus, God can send women prophets if he wishes, but we cannot send women presbyters.

Temporary factors and permanent factors

ALL these evasions and others will doubtless be in evidence once more as Anglicans debate the matter. In exposing them for what they are, however, the opponents of women's ordination are left with considerable freedom of action. They must preserve the principles of Paul's teaching, but this does not mean that they cannot adapt its application to changed cultural conditions. Paul's main concern in the three classic passages is undoubtedly that the created relationship of the sexes should be faithfully observed (1 Cor. 11: 7-9; 14: 34; 1 Tim. 2: 13f.), not that it should be expressed in any particular cultural manner. Provided, therefore, that the due relationship of the sexes is maintained, and is expressed in appropriate contemporary ways, cultural expressions of that relationship which have now passed away, such as veiling and keeping silence in public, need not be considered as any longer obligatory upon Christians. With regard to both these practices, Paul refers to contemporary custom (1 Cor. 11: 16; 14: 33, 36), and this has since changed. Today it is no disrespect to a man if a woman appears before him with her head uncovered, or opens her mouth in his presence: the very suggestion seems absurd. Indeed, at university level we are now used to women not just opening their mouths in the presence of men but teaching men, without this implying at all that they are exercising authority over those they teach. It is only when the task of teaching is combined with an authoritative office that the question of exercising authority over men comes into the picture today. The presbyterate, however, is certainly an authoritative office, as its biblical titles of *elder* and *overseer* imply, and as passages like 1 Tim. 5: 17; Heb. 13: 17, 24; 1 Pet. 5: 2f. deliberately state. Even in New Testament times, therefore, when it was normal for a congregation to have a college of elders, not a sole-pastor, the presbyterate was manifestly an authoritative office, and it could not be less so today, when there are inevitably many sole-pastorates in small congregations, and when colleges of presbyters would be expected to have a president. It would only be creating problems, not solving them, to admit women to the presbyterate but to stipulate that they must not be sole-pastors or presidents of group-pastorates, and this would in no way satisfy the protagonists of women's ordination, who regard it as 'discrimination' when women ministers are not reckoned equally eligible for the presidency of group-pastorates.[11] The same negative reaction would undoubtedly meet any suggestion that women should be admitted to the presbyterate but not to the episcopate. The straightforward and consistent course is not to admit them to the presbyterate at all.

Special cases

THE case of prophetesses, already considered, shows that the rule of the subordination of women is not a rule without exceptions. There have often, in fact, been charismatic exceptions to the rule, where God gives women a gift of leadership in the Church which cannot be denied, but which speaks for itself and does not need ordination to secure its recognition. Again, there are exceptions due to necessity. In places where women missionaries have laboured alone, because of a dearth of male missionaries, they have often been faced with the necessity of either performing for themselves ministerial tasks normally reserved to men or of letting them go by default. When they have chosen the latter option, harm has sometimes at least resulted, as when infant congregations have grown used to managing without holy communion. Archbishop Temple's idea that it would be better, in case of necessity, to authorise a deaconess to celebrate holy communion than to ordain her priest, is relevant here. Bishops could perhaps have a recognised power of dispensation in such exceptional cases. Thirdly, there are exceptions due to God's uncovenanted mercies. If the Church breaks one of God's commandments, he does not necessarily refuse all his blessings in consequence. The work of a woman presbyter is not *ipso facto* fruitless. Fourthly, we have today become used to many secular exceptions. This is not an age when the Church can give laws to the state, and to find women in positions of authority over men is a common, though not perhaps a universally accepted, feature of contemporary life. In such a situation the powers that be are still ordained of God, but the Church must set an example to the state, not conform to the state's example. It is a Christian duty to obey women in positions of secular authority. It is also a Christian duty to assist women in achieving their genuine human potentialities and rights. But a duty still remains to warn them (by example as much as by precept) against the error of usurping headship over men.

Possible lines of development

IT is not enough, however, to be negative. If it has been established that the ordination of women to the priesthood is a mistake, there still remains the important task of indicating directions in which the ministry of women can properly proceed. Since women are women not men, they have a unique ministry to perform. And since, even after all the progress of the past century and a half, there are undoubted grounds for dissatisfaction with the conditions under which the ministry of women has to be exercised today, it will not be sufficient simply to repeat what is said elsewhere about the ways in which women have exercised their ministry hitherto, but it will be necessary to indicate the points at which change and development are called for. If grounds for legitimate dissatisfaction did not exist, the tendency to claim for women admission to the presbyterate might be much less widespread than in fact it is. Having said this, one is bound to add that the situation varies somewhat from country to country and from denomination to denomination, and that what follows will apply mainly, though not exclusively, to the Church of England.

One of Hensley Henson's many provocative remarks was that 'the world wants desperately, not female priests and bishops, but Christian wives and mothers',[12] and the ministry of women will probably always remain primarily a ministry in the home. Nevertheless, as chapter two indicated, this has never been the only place where women have ministered, and it is emphatically not the only place today. There is the vocation of the female missionary. There is the call to community life, now spreading far outside Roman Catholic and Orthodox circles. There are a variety of parochial ministries, full-time and part-time, including that of the deaconess. There are the openings as Church social worker, director of religious education, trained youth leader, Sunday school organiser, chaplain's assistant, lay worker attached not to a parish but to a deanery or a team ministry, and teacher of theology. This is the sort of existing basis from which all further progress begins.

The need for development and reform is occasioned partly by the changing conditions of society and partly by defects in the inherited pattern of women's work. In either area, reform is often hindered by male conservatism and conceit.

The effects of changing conditions have been various. For one thing, the number of unmarried women has been reduced by the altered ratio of women to men in the population and by early marriage. This means that the Church must look to married women even more than it has done in the past. At the same time, now that smaller families are normal, married women are more able to take on employment outside the home, even though the burdens of housework remain considerable. This means that the Church must look to married women for more professional service and less voluntary service. Not only must offices like those of deaconess and Church Army sister be opened to married women (as they now have been), but training suitable for married women with other responsibilities must be provided.[13]

Another change is that advances in medicine are prolonging life and checking disease and debility. This offers new scope for the historic ministry of the widow.

Yet another change is that professional openings for unmarried women have vastly increased in number over the past hundred years. For a considerable time, therefore, the Church has been looking to them for professional service and not simply for voluntary service. It has not, however, made the provision for their professional service which it might have done. The lack of any security of tenure beyond three months' notice, ambiguous status, and a grudging attitude which treats their services as a second best and imposes arbitrary restrictions upon them, are hardly encouragements to the vocation of the woman parochial worker.[14]

This brings us on to the subject of defects in the inherited pattern of women's work. The basic defects here are theological. It has been pointed out by Alan Richardson that the call for the admission of women to the priesthood takes the priesthood as a fixed point, whereas the priesthood is one of the matters which needs to be rethought.[15] If the call for the admission of women to the priesthood were heeded at this stage, the problem of women's ministry would be solved only temporarily, and only for that small number of women who offered themselves for the priesthood, while the problem of the priesthood would not be solved at all.[16] Another matter which needs to be rethought is the diaconate (and with it the office of deaconess), as several recent Anglican reports on the ministry of women emphasise.[17] A third such matter is the laity. The ministry of the laity is a topic which has only recently begun to receive from theologians the attention which it deserves.[18] Everyone now knows that, according to the New Testament, all laymen have a ministry. But much more progress needs to be made in determining what that ministry is, and in making it a reality, both for men and women. At present it is still an effective argument that the only real ministry is the ordained ministry, and that consequently there can be no real ministry for women without them being ordained; and a pseudo-theological colouring is given to the argument by describing the ordained ministry as a representative priesthood, exercising the priesthood of the whole Church on the Church's behalf.[19] Further study of the ministry of the laity is the more urgent because, if all laymen have a ministry, this raises acutely the question, What is distinctive about the ministries of presbyters and deacons? Thus, not only is there a question whether women should be ordained to the presbyterate: there is also a question what the presbyterate is. Again, not only is there a question whether the deaconess is a female deacon: there is also a question what the diaconate is. In short, ministry as a whole needs a comprehensive review. Obviously, nothing of the kind can be attempted in this essay. The questions involved deserve treatises of their own, and would tend to receive different answers in different denominations. Only the most tentative answers can be given here.

There is reason to think that a comprehensive review of ministry in the Christian Church would do much more to satisfy the aspirations of women than the easy and misguided step of admitting them to the priesthood. Only a comprehensive review would take account of the gifts of all women, not just a few, and would order the ministry of the Church in a really carefully considered, permanent and well co-ordinated fashion. It is a mistake to think that Christian women are itching for the priesthood. Among parish workers, there is some frustration at restrictions of the kind listed in note 14, and at the lack of scope given in certain parishes and certain dioceses, but uncertainty seems to be more widespread than frustration. There is naturally some concern to have a more clearly defined status. There is also some desire to be able, not just to preach and baptise, but to celebrate holy communion. It is felt by a number that, within the present framework, ordination to the priesthood does seem to be the only way to the exercise of a full ministry, but it is recognised also that the present framework is under review, and that admission to the priesthood at this stage might simply delay fuller and more adequate reform. One should note that Head Deaconess Gurney has recently denied in the press that the deaconness order is 'some kind of spearhead' for the cause of ordination to the priesthood (*Church Times*, January 28th, 1972).

Although the New Testament teaches us that all Christians have their own spiritual gifts from God, and by consequence their own ministry to perform for the benefit of the whole Church, it also singles out certain ministries from others and gives them a unique status. Presbyters (or bishops) and deacons are singled out from all other ministries in a variety of places in the Acts and Epistles, qualifications are prescribed for these ministries alone, and appointment by men as well as by God is required for them (Acts 14: 23; Phil. 1: 1; 1 Tim. 3: 1-13; 5: 22; Tit. 1: 5-9; etc.). The titles *Presbyter* (or elder) and *bishop* (or overseer) imply seniority and authority in the congregation, and it is clear from this and from Acts 20:28; 1 Thes. 5:12; 1 Tim. 5:17; Heb. 13:17,24; 1 Pet. 5:2, that all other ministries are to be exercised under their guidance and rule. In addition, they have an important teaching function (1 Tim. 3: 2; 5: 17; Tit. 1: 9). Deacons (or servants), from being singled out in the same way and linked with the presbyters, but being regularly mentioned second (when mentioned at all) and bearing a less dignified title, appear to be their assistants in their ministry. Deaconesses appear to be female deacons (1 Tim. 3: 11).[20]

It may be that the office of deaconess, seen as a female deacon, and in the context of the perpetual diaconate now in process of being restored throughout the Christian Church, will go a considerable way to solve current perplexity about women's ministry. If this were to be the pattern of the future, it would not, of course, exclude a large variety of lay ministries for women, but rather assume them. Nor would it exclude ordination for women, but to an order which would work in an assistant way under the leadership of presbyters or bishops. Still less would it exclude the celibate vocation, which would be the calling of some deaconesses and of some laywomen, living either privately or in community. Whether deaconesses would work full-time or part-time is a comparatively minor question. In the New Testament, presbyters enjoy the right to have their material needs supplied (1 Tim. 5: 17f.) but are sometimes called to forego the right (Acts 20: 33-35), and the same doubtless applies to their assistants. The 1968 Lambeth Conference envisaged both deacons (whether male or female) and priests having the choice of working professionally or voluntarily (resolutions 32 and 33). The practical outworking of all this would have to be thought through and put to the test, but each of these possibilities has some claim to be allowed for in the Christian Church, and each has some contribution to make to the life of the whole body.

One aspiration which the proposals so far made would not satisfy is the desire of some women workers to be able to celebrate holy communion. The New Testament does not tie the celebration of holy communion to the episcopate or presbyterate, and ancient tradition does not do so quite as exclusively as is often supposed.[21] Certainly the ministry of the word and sacraments should normally be combined, and if deacons and deaconesses were authorised, in the absence of the priest, not only to baptise but to celebrate holy communion, this would be no greater innovation than the ordination of women to the priesthood. But the proposal would certainly be a very controversial one, and it is put forward here simply as one of the matters which would need to be considered in the comprehensive review of the Church's ministry for which we ask. It may be that as a result of such a review the aspirations of Christian women would be fully satisfied without this particular change being made.[22]

In these tentative suggestions we have looked at some of the changes that could be made in our pattern of institutional ministry. But we must, in conclusion, return to our main point that the review of ministry which is required is a comprehensive review of *all* ministry. It will therefore cover the ministry of the laity as well as the institutional ministry, and will seek to identify and distinguish the special gifts of ministry given by God to Christian men and Christian women. God made men and women different; it is perverse and, indeed, dehumanising to both sexes to pretend otherwise. Only in contexts of action into which personal qualities do not enter at all, therefore, will it be possible to treat men and women as simply interchangeable. But in the church's fellowship of mutual ministry Christians are called to be persons to each other—women, therefore, to be distinctively womanly and men distinctively manly. Nobody who ministers, whether lay or ordained, may do so as a cipher, a servant of a system whose personality is wholly sunk in his or her official role (a special twentieth century form of worldliness): such behaviour quenches the Spirit. Women's ministry must be womanly ministry. The questions to start with are: what, in Christian and personal terms, is woman? and what personal qualities and gifts of service are distinctively 'her'? and then, when these questions have been answered, it will at last become possible to reason sensibly about the order and pattern of ministry within which her gifts can best be used. But it does not appear that enquiry into these prior questions has really begun. Is it too much to hope that it may start soon?

NOTES

[1] This is not, of course, to deny that a certain amount of Roman Catholic literature in favour of the ordination of women to the priesthood has recently appeared. A good account of it may be found in *Herder Correspondence*, October 1969.

[2] W. J. Wolf, in *Journal of Ecumenical Studies*, Winter 1972, pp. 231, 235. See also Marga Bührig, 'Discrimination against Women', in *Technology and Social Justice*, ed. R. H. Preston (London, SCM, 1971).

[3] 'Some Reflections on Ecclesiastical Assemblies,' in *Theology*, May 1971, p. 209.

[4] One wonders whether this precedent will be followed in union schemes elsewhere. The Methodist Church of Great Britain, despite its decision in 1966 that women may be ordained, has hitherto refrained from ordaining them, so as to facilitate union with the Church of England. This is not in principle any different from the action of the uniting Churches in N. India when they withdrew recognition from their women ministers in order to make the Church of North India possible. What will now happen about the union schemes in the USA and New Zealand, where the Anglicans have so recently reaffirmed the Anglican position on the ordination of women?

[5] The preparation of this report was the occasion of Professor von Allmen's letter to her, which constitutes chapter nine of the present work.

[6] On Gal. 3: 28, see the essays by G. G. Blum and Hans Cavallin.

[7] For the latest statement of this objection, see G. B. Caird, 'Paul and Women's Liberty' (*Bulletin of the John Rylands Library*, Spring 1972), which Dr. Caird kindly lent to the writers in proof form.
[8] See Joachim Jeremias, *Jerusalem in the Time of Jesus* (London, SCM, 1969), pp. 358-363; Alfred Edersheim, *Sketches of Jewish Social Life in the Days of Christ*, 1876, p. 154.
[9] *Beauty and Bands* (London, Hodder and Stoughton, 1955), pp. 179, 186f.
[10] See Michael Bruce's essay.
[11] See Brigalia Bam, *What is Ordination Coming To?* (Geneva, WCC, 1971), p. 78.
[12] *Bishoprick Papers* (London, OUP, 1946), p. 10.
[13] See *Women in Ministry* (London, CIO, 1968), pp. 56-58.
[14] See *Women in Ministry, passim.* Remuneration has improved in the Church of England in the last decade, but arbitrary restrictions remain. Instances are the permission to read some non-sacramental services but not others, the permission to preach on some occasions but not at the Holy Communion service, and the withholding of permission to distribute the elements at that service. Most of these restrictions are in process of being removed by the further revision of Canon D1 now before the General Synod, assuming that diocesan bishops will take full advantage of it.
[15] In *Women and Holy Orders* (London, CIO, 1966), p. 125f.
[16] There is no reason to think that the number of women offering themselves for the priesthood would be very large. The experience of Congregationalists is here instructive. A distinguished Congregational theologian, Nathaniel Micklem, points out that, though they have admitted women to ordination for many years, there is little demand for women ministers, and only with the greatest difficulty do they receive a 'call' from a congregation (*Congregationalism and Episcopacy*, London, Independent Press, 1951, p. 18f.). Where the number ordained and called is larger, the reason can be of the worst kind. The Remonstrant Church of Holland is said to have found it necessary to stop ordaining women because congregations were calling women to their pastorates rather than men simply in order to get a minister at a cheaper rate.
[17] *Women and Holy Orders*, pp. 32-37; *Women in Ministry*, pp. 39-50.
[18] See, for example, Michael Green, *Called to Serve* (London, Hodder and Stoughton, 1964), ch. 2; J. R. W. Stott, *One People* (London, Falcon Books, 1969); and the literature there cited.
[19] This is the theory of R. C. Moberly. For a consideration of it, see J. I. Packer's essay, and chapter two in R. T. Beckwith, *Priesthood and Sacraments* (Marcham Manor Press, 1964).
[20] It must be remembered, however, that Dr. Blum does not interpret 1 Tim. 3: 11 of deaconesses but of deacons' wives, and that Dr. Hardy holds that even in Rom. 16: 1 the title *deaconess* is purely honorific.
[21] See *Didache* 10; Tertullian, *Exhortation to Chastity* 7; Hippolytus, *Apostolic Tradition* 10: 1f.
[22] The writers of this essay are indebted to a number of ladies engaged in training women workers and in supervising women's work, but who prefer to remain anonymous, for much helpful information about women's work and women's views. The responsibility for the proposals that the essay makes lies wholly with the authors, however.

The Christian World of C. S. Lewis

by Professor Clyde Kilby
Casebound £1.50   Paperback 75p

Here is the first study of C. S. Lewis as a Christian apologist. Professor Kilby analyses Lewis's Christian impact, his ideas, and the appeal to ordinary readers which so few other Christian writers today have achieved.

Reviewers said

The central emphases of Lewis's teaching are lucidly expounded and his achievement as a Christian apologist is justly assessed.   **British Book News.**

Professor Kilby's book will interest all who have been influenced by C. S. Lewis.   **Theology.**

A valuable help to the understanding of Lewis's thought and life.   **Time and Tide.**

Marcham Books, Appleford, Abingdon, Berks.